# WEMYSS WARE

## a decorative Scottish Pottery

Presented by Victoria de Rin
and David Macmillan

Written by Peter Davis
and Robert Rankine

1986

## SCOTTISH ACADEMIC PRESS

EDINBURGH AND LONDON

Published by
Scottish Academic Press Ltd,
33 Montgomery Street
Edinburgh EH7 5JX

SBN 7073 0354 0

British Library Cataloguing in Publication Data

Wemyss Ware: a decorative Scottish pottery
I. Wemyss ware
I. Davis, P. and Rankine R.
738.3'7   NK4340 W4

ISBN 0 7073 0354 0

Photography Michael Maclaren

Design John McWilliam

Printed and bound in Great Britain
by Clark Constable, Edinburgh and London

THIS BOOK IS
RESPECTFULLY DEDICATED TO
HER MAJESTY QUEEN ELIZABETH
THE QUEEN MOTHER

Her Majesty Queen Elizabeth The Queen Mother accepting a Wemyss
Goblet, produced by Rogers de Rin to honour her 80th birthday.
The Presentation was made by Pamela, Countess of Mansfield, at Scone
Palace in August 1980. The goblet raised a substantial contribution to the
Stars' Organisation for Spastics.

Photograph by Cowper, Perth

Probably the most important piece of Wemyss to come under the hammer so far.
A tureen and cover modelled as a Carp, 18½" long. Sold at Sotheby's in February 1984 for over £3,600 to the Wemyss specialists, Rogers de Rin. The Carp is now in the collection of Huntly House Museum, Edinburgh.

# FOREWORD

I am delighted to have been asked by Victoria de Rin to provide this foreword to a long-needed book. I wish I had had it some fourteen years ago when beginning to catalogue in Sotheby's ceramics department and finding myself with a black and white cat to describe. Never having heard of Wemyss, I assumed it to be Continental, probably Dutch. I was soon disabused.

Professor Davis and Robert Rankine have been researching the history of the factory over eighteen years and the depth of their probing, which included hundreds of meetings, conversations and exchanges of correspondence with those involved with the Fife Pottery shows in their scholarly text. Entirely appropriate to the subject, it is written in a light-hearted and readable way in which their enthusiasm for the subject is obvious. Nevertheless, Peter Davis' keen mind as a botanist and author of international standing has stamped the text with an authority which should lay to rest forever some of the apocryphal stories and misconceptions long associated with the factory.

Working with David Macmillan, Victoria has pursued the long but exciting task of tracking down what seems to be the almost infinite variety of form and painted decoration, organizing the photography and co-ordinating the project.

Douglas Grant and The Scottish Academic Press are to be congratulated on publishing what should stand for many years as the definitive work on Wemyss.

DAVID BATTIE
Director of Sotheby's European
Ceramics and Glass Department

# CONTENTS

# PREFACE

Wemyss Ware was one of the products of Robert Heron & Son, The Fife Pottery, Gallatown – now part of Kirkcaldy in the Kingdom of Fife. It was made from c.1882–1930. The bold and distinctive decoration of this ware has its detractors and its enthusiastic devotees, the latter having to dig ever more deeply into their pockets to satisfy a craving for possession. Wanting, but being unable to have, someone else's Wemyss can be a most frustrating experience.

Wemyss was a vigorous, back-to-nature movement with nothing in common with the Pre–Raphaelites or Art Nouveau. Usually painted on homely shapes, the decoration achieved a pleasing balance between the under-glaze decoration and the whiteness of the pot. Flowers, fruits, birds and animals were its main subjects, bringing the garden, orchard and farmyard into the house. To see a display of Wemyss on a dull day is to be dazzled by its brightness – as though the sun has come out.

The name for Wemyss Ware seems to have been taken from the Wemyss family of neighbouring Wemyss Castle, who continued to take a keen amateur interest in its development, just as the Countess of Dunmore had done in the development of Dunmore Ware. The name and unofficial association with the Wemyss family evidently helped the new ware to receive a very favourable reception. The name Wemyss is from the Gaelic *uamh*, meaning cave; in the cliffs below Wemyss Castle are the famous Wemyss caves in which are ancient or Pictish markings on the rock face. (cf. Moncrieffe of that Ilk and David Hicks, *The Highland Clans*, p. 47. Publ. Barrie & Rockliff, 1967).

Although Wemyss Ware (after a short, self-coloured period) was exuberantly decorative, much of it was not very durable: it cracked and broke too easily. Nevertheless, Wemyss probably played a considerable part in a leisured dowager's day. With it she could have taken her morning tea in bed, washed or bathed, curled her hair and powdered her nose, tucked into porridge, honey or marmalade for breakfast, dealt with her correspondence with the aid of inkstands and paper-racks, used a delightful dessert service and taken a lavish afternoon tea – including muffins. At the end of the day she could have chosen a suitable Wemyss candle-stick and tottered up to bed. If she had taken a drop too much, she might have stubbed her foot on a pig door-stop and soaked her poor old feet in a rose footbath. It may not have been a very useful day, but with breakages common it was quite a profitable one for the Fife Pottery and their famous London agent, Thos. Goode & Co. of South Audley Street.

We have been able to trace few written records and no correspondence or diaries concerning the Fife Pottery or the people who worked there. All we have are an early Price List (1855), two catalogues, an Inventory of Robert Heron's house and harbour records for the import of clay. We have therefore had to lean heavily on the Census records, and the records of births, marriages and deaths, together with Robert Heron's Will, some extracts from the Pottery Gazette (London), local Kirkcaldy newspapers of the time, and statements made to us since the mid-1960's by people connected with the Fife Pottery in its last years. In particular, our numerous discussions with the late J. K. MacKenzie, who had been at the Fife Pottery since boyhood and was its Manager from 1920–1927, have provided us with a particularly useful source of recorded information which we were able to check with him on successive visits to Kirkcaldy.

It must be pointed out here that the early history of the Fife Pottery (c.1790–1930) is entwined with that of the nearby Kirkcaldy (Links) Pottery of David Methven & Son. The chronology of this intricate relationship is summarised by Robert Rankine on p. 49 (Chapter XII).

# ACKNOWLEDGMENTS

The authors owe much to the kindness and hospitality of Wemyss collectors and thank them for placing at our disposal pieces for photography that would be otherwise inaccessible.

We have enjoyed support and encouragement from many people and would like to thank all those who have contributed material, their time, knowledge or advice.

Her Majesty The Queen

Her Majesty Queen Elizabeth The Queen Mother

The Chairman and Directors of Sotheby's for a generous contribution to photography

The Scottish Arts Council

Philip Wilson Publishers Limited

Lady Abdy
Captain Alistair Aird
The Dowager Countess of Airlie
Lord and Lady Airlie
The Duke of Athol
Mr. David Battie
Mrs. Katherine Bayne
Mr. John Brooke-Little
Mrs. P. Campbell-Blythe
Mr. William G. Carslake
Mrs. Shiela Castle

Mrs. Tessa de Chair
Miss Nan Clark
Mr. and Mrs. Cooper
Mrs. Kay Dickson
Lord and Lady Dunluce
Captain and Mrs. Ranald Farquharson
Mr. Patrick Feeny
Mrs. Iris Fox
Dr. George Fraser
Lady Carina Frost
Mr. Jack Fudge
Mr. George Gibb
Hon. Hugh Gibson
Lord and Lady Glenconner
Mr. and Mrs. Goodbody
Mr. Garry Grant
Thomas Goode and Co.
The Misses Greenaway
Mr. John Greig
Mr. Derek Hill
Mr. John Hill
Mr. and Mrs. Hugh Hutchinson
Miss Hazel Hutchinson
Mrs. Anne Jackson
Mrs. Pauline Jamieson
Dr. and Mrs. George Laird
The Earl and Countess of Mansfield
Mr. and Mrs. A. J. MacDonald-Buchanan
Mrs. Marion McInnes
Mrs. Morag Macmillan
The Rev. G. Mackenzie
Mr. and Mrs. David McAlpine
Mr. David Methven
Dr. and Mrs. Morrow-Brown
Mr. John May

Mrs. Elizabeth Nekola
Mr. and Mrs. K. Nekola
Miss Mariebell Nekola
Mr. Sandy Ness
Hon. James Ogilvy
Hon. Mrs. June Ogilvy
Mr. Stuart Piepenstock
Professor Sir John Plumb
Mrs. Susan Proctor
Mr. Neil Read
Miss Joy Rennie
Mr. and Mrs. William Robb
Mrs. Joan Rothenburg
Mr. Eric D. Sandland
Mr. Kenneth Southall
Mrs. J. Steer
The Countess of Sutherland
Mrs. Woroniecki
Mrs. Esther Weekes
Lady Victoria Wemyss
Mr. John R. Williamson
Mr. Philip Wilson

Huntly House Museum:
      Mr. H. Coutts (Curator)
Kirkcaldy Museum and Art Gallery:
      Miss Andrea Kerr (Curator)
The Keeper of the Records, Scottish Record Office, Edinburgh
The Registrar General, General Register Office, Edinburgh
National Library of Scotland, Edinburgh
Kirkcaldy Public Library
Clackmannan County Library
London Museum

The story of Wemyss Ware and
of the people who made it.

# I. THE FIFE POTTERY IN ITS SCOTTISH CONTEXT

Before the advent of Wemyss Ware in Fife, the Glasgow potteries and their satellites were already in artistic decline, producing a vast amount of transfer-printed ware that varied from pleasing to mundane. The largest and best-known firm was that of J. and M. P. Bell & Co. which was producing white earthenware from c.1842–c.1910. By the 1880's the Glasgow potteries seem to have run short of ideas, though it must be admitted that they still produced an attractive array of transfer-printed milk jugs, dinner ware etc.

Some of the East Coast potteries followed a very different and more inventive path. Two, apart from the Fife Pottery, are particularly relevant to our subject: the Dunmore Pottery in Stirlingshire and the Kirkcaldy Pottery of David Methven & Son, both of which show, in part of their range, strong stylistic connections with the Wemyss Ware of Robert Heron & Son.

The Dunmore Pottery was run by Peter Gardner from c.1866 (his father died in December of that year) and benefited from the patronage and ideas of the Countess of Dunmore who lived in Dunmore Park near Airth in Stirlingshire. The local red clay was initially used, but later replaced by white clay. The shapes varied from simple to intricate, many being characterised by their lustrous treacley glazes; the earlier pieces were probably monochrome, the later ones mottled or splashed under glaze. Some of the earlier undecorated

Wemyss Ware from the Fife Pottery has evidently been copied from Dunmore, the shapes and even the colours being similar or identical. Fortunately the latter ware is impressed 'Dunmore' or 'Peter Gardner, Dunmore Pottery', and can thus be distinguished from early self-coloured Wemyss, which bore an impressed Wemyss mark and often a number.

The other East Coast Pottery that produced ware similar to Wemyss was the Kirkcaldy Pottery (known in earlier times as the 'Links Pottery') of David Methven & Son, situated only three miles from Heron's works. All the East Coast potteries, including Bo'ness and Alloa, produced a mass of sponge ware (including carpet bowls), the designs being dabbed onto the biscuit prior to firing, using the cut and shaped roots of sponges. The owners of the potteries in Kirkcaldy, connected by marriage until 1892, appear to have been on terms of friendly rivalry. Heron's well planned Pottery, though smaller than Methven's, was considered a cut above the latter, being more ambitious and refined in the quality of its ware, both in regard to the body of the pot and style of decoration.

MacKenzie told us that the clays used for Wemyss Ware (and earthenware manufacture generally) came up by sea from S.W. England: china clay from Cornwall, two kinds of ball clay (one from Devon, the other from Dorset), and purple stone from Cornwall. Calcified flint was added to give colour and resist sudden temperature changes. A small quantity of cobalt chloride was used as a body stain to whiten the clay. Messrs Heron fritted their own glaze, and

Robert M. Heron and his sister Jessie C. Heron, c.1894.

ground it with lead in an Alsing cylinder. For technical terms used in the pottery industry, see F. Hamer, *The Potter's Dictionary of Materials and Techniques* (Pitman & Black, 1975). On their return journey the boats took back coal from Fife.

When Mary Methven Heron died in 1887, the Fife Pottery passed to her son Robert

Methven Heron and his sister Jessie. The Pottery House was well appointed, and they appear to have lived there in some style. Heron was evidently a popular and convivial man who enjoyed entertaining his friends. He was considered a 'bit of a lad', being apt to slip off to Paris from time to time. J. Arnold Fleming (*Scottish Pottery*, p. 198, 1923) tells us that Heron 'was well known in London, where he was as much esteemed as in his native town as an able and artistic potter'. An inventory compiled after his death may sound an uncompromising start, but 20 pages listing c.600 items provide many clues to what life was like at the Pottery House in Heron's day.

The drawing room was large and well-furnished. There were a considerable number of pictures (oils and watercolours of landscapes, seascapes, cattle, game and girls). Wemyss (including a footbath) was present. At least in Jessie's time it was an hospitable and musical household. There was a walnut cottage piano, an American organ, a violin and an accordion. There was also a card table, a double-barrelled gun (which may have accounted for the stuffed fox in the hall), golf clubs and a croquet set. A striking feature of the inventory is the wide range of cutlery, china, glass and crystal. There were (for instance) 17 hock glasses, 14 rummers, 19 champagne glasses, 35 sherry glasses, a dozen bottles of champagne and supply of Glengarnock Whisky.

The garden contained a greenhouse in which Heron presumably grew some of the plants that figure in Wemyss Ware. He kept a coachman, a landau and a 'brown horse'. These were involved in an amusing incident recounted to us in Kirkcaldy. One night Heron was kept awake by persistent hiccups – hardly surprising when you consider his well stocked cellar. He sent his coachman round to bring back his physician, Dr. Proudfoot, so that the latter could effect a cure. The coachman, however, returned without the doctor, and handed Heron a disconcertingly short prescription: 'Go to Hell!' The hiccups promptly stopped.

According to an obituary notice in *The Fife Free Press* (30 June 1906), Robert Heron 'had a serious attack of Angina Pectoris' about the beginning of June 'which reduced him greatly and this was followed by another attack two days before his death' on 23 June. The obituary continues 'Mr. Heron was greatly esteemed in the district where he had resided all his lifetime, and he did many acts of charity to the poor and aged which he never liked to be known. While taking no active part in public affairs he always took a great interest in the welfare and prosperity of his native town.'

Besides many legacies of a personal nature, Heron in his will bequeathed the following sums of money to charitable organisations: £200 to Kirkcaldy Cottage Hospital; £100 to Rev. J. C. Bell of Pathhead Parish Church 'to be distributed by him amongst the necessitous poor in such a manner as he may in his absolute discretion think best'; and £500 for Prevention of Cruelty to Animals. The residue of his estate, including the Fife Pottery, was left to his friend William Williamson. The largest bequests were to Charles Grey Wotherspoon of Hillside, Aberdour, £1,000; and to Ann, Elizabeth, Isabella and Margaret Brown (presumably young ladies) of Ivy Lodge, £1,000. To his Business Manager at the Fife Pottery, J. K. MacKenzie (senior), he left £500; to Peter Weepers, Manager, £100; to John McKinnon, Mould Maker, £50; and to Karel Nekola, Artist, £50. This might imply that Heron's excellent mould maker and his chief decorator were considered of equal status.

On his death Robert Heron had left the Fife Pottery to William Williamson who was in business on his own as a linen merchant and obviously a close friend of Robert Heron who, when he died, had relatives still living (he left money to his cousin, Mary Methven, to buy a mourning ring). The Williamson family did not become directly involved in running the Pottery which was managed on their behalf by James MacKenzie, Heron's former Business Manager, together with an Accountant from Williamson's business named Joseph Greenaway. James MacKenzie was succeeded by his son Kenneth.

## II. ESTABLISHING WEMYSS WARE

The brothers Archibald and Andrew Gray probably set up business as potters in Gallatown around 1812 but by c.1817 the buildings were too small for their expanding business. They erected a large new pottery on a site leased from

Karel Nekola and Isabella, his wife, c.1885.

the Earl of Rosslyn which they named The Fife Pottery. The lease, registered on 9 January 1821, is for ground on which the Grays had 'lately built a Pottery'. On 14 February 1822 the Company had to raise a loan of £600 from the Glasgow Banking Co. but unfortunately Andrew Gray died a few years later and Gray & Co. were declared bankrupt on 21 March 1826. Some idea of the scale of this pottery business can be gauged from the bankruptcy papers which have survived, for by 1826 the Company was heavily in debt. They owed in addition to the money borrowed from the Glasgow Bank, £314 to the National Bank of Scotland, £125 to the Commercial Bank, £302 to the Fife Banking Co., together with smaller sums to individuals, dealers and merchants not only in the east of Scotland but also in York, London, Burslem and Glasgow. The Company's assets included earthenware and work in hand worth £610, pottery materials to value of £219, bricks and tiles valued at £587, and rags and old iron at £138 together with many other items. When the affairs of Gray & Co. were finally settled the creditors received payment at a rate of 4/6d (22½p) in the pound.

The new pottery was large and well planned. Over a hundred and forty years later it was described to us by J. K. MacKenzie, formerly manager, as 'an exceptionally well laid out factory obviously planned by people who understood well the workings of a production pottery'. Among the earliest known marked examples of the ware from those early days are a pair of rectangular wall plaques showing a bust,

in relief, of King George IV and dated 10 May 1826. The plaques, issued to commemorate the visit to Edinburgh of George IV in 1822, are incised 'Fife Pottery' and are currently on view at the Glasgow Museum and Art Gallery, Kelvingrove.

Production probably carried on during the sequestration of Gray & Co., possibly under the supervision of John Methven of the Links Pottery, for by 1827 he had bought the Fife Pottery from the Receiver, taking over, too, the burden of the loan from the Glasgow Banking Co. During the decade which followed, the two potteries in the Kirkcaldy district were owned and managed by John Methven aided by his only son David and by his son-in-law Robert Heron. Tragedy struck this family in 1837: both father and son died in that year, David in March and John four months later in August. John Methven left his pottery businesses to his daughter Mary and her husband Robert Heron; they soon sold the Links Pottery to Mary's uncle, George Methven, who had inherited the Methven Brick and Tile works which adjoined it.

This left Robert Heron free to concentrate his energies on developing and expanding the Fife Pottery. The debt owed to the Glasgow Bank continued to be a drag on the Pottery, and so little profit was made over the years that settlement was not reached until 21 May 1885, when the younger Robert Heron paid over the sum of £450 'in final discharge of Bond of Credit and Disposition of Security dated 14 February 1822 on the Glasgow Bank Co.'

## The DEVELOPMENT OF POTTERIES IN KIRKCALDY

The history of the Fife Pottery was closely connected with the Kirkcaldy (or Links) Pottery of David Methven & Sons. These two potteries were about three miles apart. Their history, involving changes of name and ownership, makes an interesting narrative and we have tried to present the main facts here as simply as we can. The full chronology appears on page 49.

| | | | |
|---|---|---|---|
| 1714 | Adam and Robertson Brick and Tile Works in the Linkton of Abbotshall. | c.1790 | Gallatown Pottery |
| 1776 | Bought by David Methven. | 1817 | Built large new works called 'The Fife Pottery'. |
| c.1809 | **John Methven** makes pottery in a building adjacent to the Brick and Tile Works. | 1826 | Sold due to bankruptcy. |
| 1827 | At death David Methven's property is left as follows:<br>(i) John Methven gets his land on which his pottery is built<br>(ii) Brick and Tile Works pass to George Methven. | c.1827 | Bought by **John Methven**. |

**1837**  **John Methven** leaves both potteries to Robert & Mary Heron.

| | | | |
|---|---|---|---|
| 1837 | George Methven buys Links Pottery from the Herons. At his death (ten years later) he leaves both the Links Pottery and the Brick and Tile Works to his nephew David Methven (III). | c.1882 | Karel Nekola appointed decorator at the Fife Pottery. |
| 1864 | After death of David Methven, ownership of Links Pottery and the Brick and Tile Works passes to his son James. | 1887 | Robert Methven Heron and his sister Jessie inherit the Fife Pottery from their mother. |
| 1887 | James Methven takes Andrew Young (his pottery manager) into partnership. Name was changed to **'The Kirkcaldy Pottery'**. | 1906 | Robert Heron dies and William Williamson (flax merchant) inherits the Fife Pottery. |
| | | 1915 | Karel Nekola dies. |
| 1892 | Andrew Young and his sons buy the Kirkcaldy Pottery and the Brick and Tile Works. | 1916 | Edwin Sandland appointed chief decorator. |
| 1915 | Andrew Young dies and leaves the Kirkcaldy Pottery to his sons. | 1928 | Edwin Sandland dies and Joseph Nekola takes over as chief decorator. |

**1930**  **Both Potteries close**

Robert Heron, junior, found it possible to pay off this debt, not from the profits of the Fife Pottery (nor from the new Wemyss Ware), but probably as a result of a substantial legacy.

Godden, in his *Encyclopaedia of British Pottery and Porcelain Marks* (1964), lists as unidentified the marks J. M. & Co. and J. M. & Son, both of which occur on blue printed earthenware from the 1830–45 period. These are almost certainly the marks of John Methven's Potteries at this period. Some time after 1837 Robert Heron began trading under his own name, for by 1855 a Price List was issued headed 'Robert Heron, Fife Pottery' (cf. p. 42). This shows the firm to be producing standard ranges of table and kitchen ware in cream and with blue-edged, sponged and transfer printed decoration; also in 'flowing colours' (probably red, green and blue). In addition the firm produced the inevitable chimney ornaments beloved by Victorian cottagers, such as dogs, cats and cockerels, together with a successful line in gilded and enamelled 'Rosslyn jet'. Apart from local sales the main outlets for most of these productions were the Colonies. The Fife Pottery appears to have sold strongly to Australian, African and Canadian markets (cf. R. W. Finlayson, *Portneuf Pottery*, publ. Longmans, Canada, 1972).

It was on this foundation of pottery experience and tradition that the younger Robert Heron began, probably in the early 1870's, to plan and develop a line in more sophisticated, decorated ware. To begin with he applied underglaze polychrome decoration of fruits, flowers and birds to his standard range of teapots and cheese stands (some of the latter with rustic handles, oak leaves and acorns), punch bowls etc. These are usually lightly gilded and bear such decorations as grapes, plums, apples, brambles; convolvulus, pyrethrum, daffodils, dog roses with a bee; swallows, robins, herons and stags. By the mid-1880's Heron had refined the ware to the superior (but ungilded) Wemyss Ware which captured the market and continues to delight collectors today.

The success of decorated Wemyss Ware in the late Victorian-Edwardian period was largely due to the guiding hand of Robert Heron and the skill of a Czech decorator, Karel Nekola, born in Svetla, Bohemia, in c.1857. It seems likely that Heron deliberately sought out a gifted decorator to develop this ware and give it an edge over his competitors. Nekola was brought over from the Continent (possibly from Dresden) and was no doubt glad to escape being drafted into the Austro-Hungarian Army. Accompanying him, or brought over about the same time, were several other continental craftsmen. Knowing no English, they found life in Kirkcaldy distinctly uncongenial, and very soon returned to the Continent. Nekola, however, knew some English when he came and, undismayed, set about training a small team of local underglaze decorators. In the absence of written records it is difficult to establish exact dates. We do know, however, that at least two German decorators, William Starich, aged 24 and August Pasche, aged 19, were living in the Parish of Dysart at the time of the national census in March 1881, Starich being then employed as a pottery gilder and Pasche as a pottery printer. It is our considered opinion that they were two of a group, brought over from Bohemia by Robert Heron c.1880, which included among its number Karel Nekola (in his native country, Karla Nekoly). That Nekola was already established in the Fife Pottery by 1883 is confirmed by the existence of a pair of plaques showing local scenes, one of which is signed and dated by him in that year. The 1891 census (Parish of Dysart, Kirkcaldy) records him as a naturalised British subject. He was a handsome man, dark haired and with charming manners. Soon after his arrival in Gallatown he courted Robert Heron's cook, Isabella Thomson, and they were married on 8 July 1884 – an arrangement no doubt advantageous to Heron as it ensured the retention of his top decorator. From the marriage register we learn that Karel Nekola was a bachelor aged 26 years, employed as a pottery painter and designer. The Nekolas settled down at 1 Rosslyn Street, near the Fife Pottery, and raised a family of five.

Thanks to recent researches, the beginning of marked Wemyss Ware can be safely pushed back to the autumn of 1882. An article in *The Fifeshire Advertiser* of 28 October, 1882 reads as follows: 'We have had an opportunity this week to examine this new ware, manufactured by Robert Heron & Son at the Fife Pottery, Gallatown.' We can plausibly conclude that Wemyss Ware was probably on view in October of that year. It is to be noted that the article in *The Fifeshire Advertiser* concentrates on describing shapes and glazes and has very little to say about painted decoration. It states that 'The designs are taken from old ware in possession of the Wemyss family of Wemyss Castle . . . some being of the most curious shapes imaginable – round, square and diamond-shaped. There are a few of the same ware of light and graceful Grecian outline, rounded and more like the remains of Tuscan pottery, while others still resemble no vessels of which we are at all familiar.' We have seen undated coloured plates advertising Methven's ware which illustrates classical shapes similar to those described above – apparently a potential rival.

On Wemyss glazes, the same issue of *The Fifeshire Advertiser* goes on to say that 'the articles are made in two colours – deep fleshy red and a yellow, *each piece having one colour only*. . . . The ware is sure to be a favourite with people of taste, as few things could be more beautiful for, say, the decoration of a main entrance. The Messrs. Heron have also tried the ware with great success for smaller vessels of different

Wemyss Castle, 1903.

kinds, such as various bowls, candlesticks, cups and other ancient looking articles, which, though doubtful as to their particular use, are extremely effective as decoration. These are made in the two colours mentioned, and a few in green.' Only at the end of the article is modest decoration mentioned: 'several are painted in two colours, the patterns being copied from the old ware in Wemyss Castle'.

*The Pottery Gazette* (pp. 462–463) of 1 May 1883 contains the following contributions (our italics): 'One of our east country houses, Robert Heron & Son, in addition to turning out very good painted and gilt jet ware [Rosslyn jet] in the shape of cheese stands, teapots etc., has been *devoting attention to ornamenting and painting on a more ambitious scale* than is usual among Scottish Potters. Several specimens of their vases, of large size and nicely modelled shapes, which the author saw recently in one of our leading shops, were exceedingly creditable to the makers both in design and finish.' From this we can assume that decorated Wemyss was being produced at the Fife Pottery by the spring of 1883. It seems likely that Lady Henry Grosvenor, of Wemyss Castle, encouraged this new development.

On 1 October 1883 *The Pottery Gazette* (p. 956) had this to say: 'One might be allowed to wonder why the well known energy and business capabilities of our Glasgow and west country houses actually appear to be dormant and moribund, as the east coast houses may be credited with the starting and development of all fresh wares in late years . . . and last but not least the WEMYSS WARE of Robert Heron &

18

Son of Kirkcaldy. This latter ware, if I am not mistaken, *had its inception from some distinguished local amateurs* and under the fostering care and attention of the late manager of the firm, Mr. Robert McLaughlan, who died unfortunately two weeks ago, it has reached its present commanding distinction. The models are nearly all antique and with a very good glaze, first class finish, moderate prices and high patronage, it is sure to conduce both to the credit and profit of the firm . . .' It would seem that Robert Heron and his manager, McLaughlan, were primarily responsible for the establishment of Wemyss Ware and that influential patronage from Wemyss Castle set it off to a swinging start.

From the abstracts quoted above we can conclude (1) that marked Wemyss Ware started off as a self-coloured ware in competition with Dunmore and Methven; (2) that painted decoration (still accompanied by some self-coloured ware) soon became the dominant Wemyss line and was to sweep the board with its competitors. It must be pointed out, however, that even in its heyday Wemyss was only a small proportion of the Pottery's total output.

# III. MANAGEMENT, POTTING & FIRING

A good general account of the processes involved in pottery production is given in Arnold Fleming's Scottish Pottery (1923, re-printed 1973), but here we are concerned with more restricted aspects – Wemyss as it was produced at the Fife Pottery. For the layman (and the authors) this is a tricky and technical subject, hard to visualise, and one which we can only deal with rather briefly, illustrating the management structure and citing some examples of Wemyss pots made by three major processes.

## 1. MANAGEMENT:

The management of the Fife Pottery was inevitably a practical and hierarchical one. The accompanying diagram illustrates its structure:

A ground plan on page 20 shows the layout of the Pottery as it was before being demolished in c.1956. As the buildings to the south and east, including the kilns, were presumably destroyed before this plan was drawn, their position is only roughly indicated here. The aerial view of the Pottery (p. 23) was taken before demolition and shows clearly the four bottle-necked kilns and other salient features.

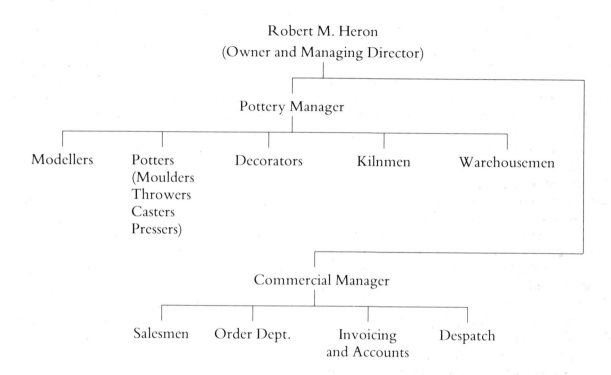

## 2. POTTING:

It must be said that MacKenzie had a poor opinion of potting techniques at the Fife Pottery in comparison with those employed at Staffordshire. However, as he admitted, the lower fired biscuit made life easier for the decorators. Wemyss Ware is appreciated, not for fine potting, but for its underglaze decoration and glittering glaze.

The following notes exemplify the three ways in which most Wemyss Ware was potted: A. *Thrown Wemyss* included Mugs (with 1, 2 or 3 handles), Japan Vases, Grosvenor Vases (later moulded), Lady Eva Vases, Loving Cups, Spill Vases, Canterbury Jugs and Teapots. The firm's best thrower was Robert Hay, probably at the Pottery from the beginning of Wemyss until at least 1906. The characteristic handles of the mugs were fashioned through a wad box and their ends pressed onto the side of the mug with slip. The heavier handles of Loving Cups were more elaborately moulded. As unmarked Methven mugs can be mistaken for those of Wemyss, it should be pointed out that the handles of Methven mugs project at a rather wide angle and have rounded margins. In contrast the characteristic handles of Wemyss

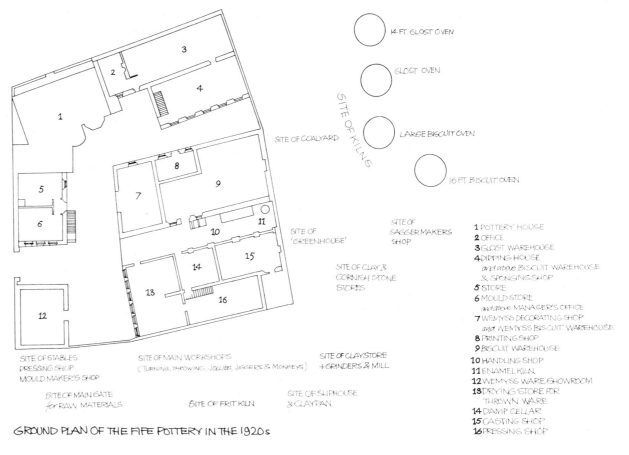

Robert Methven Heron and William Williamson, c.1900

GROUND PLAN OF THE FIFE POTTERY IN THE 1920s

14-FT. GLOST OVEN

GLOST OVEN

LARGE BISCUIT OVEN

16 FT BISCUIT OVEN

SITE OF KILNS

SITE OF COALYARD

SITE OF 'GREENHOUSE'

SITE OF SAGGER MAKERS SHOP

SITE OF CLAY & CORNISH STONE STORES

SITE OF STABLES
PRESSING SHOP
MOULD MAKER'S SHOP

SITE OF MAIN WORKSHOPS
(TURNING, THROWING, JOLLIES, JIGGERS & MONKEYS)

SITE OF CLAYSTORE
+ GRINDERS & MILL

SITE OF MAIN GATE
for RAW MATERIALS

SITE OF FRIT KILN

SITE OF SLIPHOUSE
& CLAYPAN

1 POTTERY HOUSE
2 OFFICE
3 GLOST WAREHOUSE
4 DIPPING HOUSE
   and above BISCUIT WAREHOUSE
   & SPONGING SHOP
5 STORE
6 MOULD STORE
   and above MANAGER'S OFFICE
7 WEMYSS DECORATING SHOP
   and WEMYSS BISCUIT WAREHOUSE
8 PRINTING SHOP
9 BISCUIT WAREHOUSE
10 HANDLING SHOP
11 ENAMEL KILN
12 WEMYSS WARE SHOWROOM
13 DRYING STORE FOR
   THROWN WARE
14 DAMP CELLAR
15 CASTING SHOP
16 PRESSING SHOP

mugs usually project at a narrower angle and the margins are rather sharp.

B. *Moulded (pressed) Wemyss* was largely the work of Heron's very able mould-maker, John McKinnon, who collaborated with Jessie Heron on the modelling. The modelling of the pots for the Fife Pottery was of a fairly high standard, avoiding the worst excesses of the late Victorian era. Indeed many of the pots from the general range of wares were successfully decorated for the Wemyss range. Those items, specially modelled for the new ware, were designed with clean and pleasing lines and could pass as 'modern' today. The Teacup and Saucer (Plate 73b), Ewer and Basin (Plate 101) and the Preserve Jars (Plate 239) are examples of this simple but stylish designing which continued until Robert Heron's death in 1906. Thereafter design standards seemed to slip and a few unfortunate shapes entered the catalogues.

The moulds were generally made in halves, lined with clay and then pressed together before the clay dried. The following example is of a Wemyss Pig (large or small). This is bisected horizontally into two unequal sections, the lower half and a front leg being part of the lower mould; the upper half required two moulded ears and a back leg to be smoothly joined on to the body; the curly tail was put on last. These procedures, of course, had to be carried out with the use of slip while the clay was still pliant. Other moulded pieces of Wemyss included slender candlesticks (bisected vertically), Combe Flower Pots, Ewers, Heart Inkstands, Kenmore Vases, Geese Flower Holders, Baskets, Sailor Jugs and Cats – the bisection running into the latter's ears. Lady Eva Vases (initially thrown) were later moulded.

C. *Cast Wemyss.* According to MacKenzie, casting was introduced surprisingly late at the Fife Pottery: in Sandland's time, c.1920–22. A feature of cast ware is that it is relatively lightweight, lacking the spiral markings inside (often partially sponged out) that we associate with thrown Wemyss. Examples of cast ware included Biscuit Barrels, low preserve jar fruit knob, tall mugs, sugar bowls, the later cups and saucers, and the Leven Vase (according to MacKenzie the last Wemyss shape to be introduced at the Fife Pottery).

3. FIRING:

Decorated Wemyss could never be fired at the recommended temperature – that would have been far too hot. The brilliant colouring of Wemyss decoration could only be obtained if the biscuit ware, after painting and dipping in the clear glaze, was given its second firing in the sheltered part of the kilns, where it was protected in fireclay saggars (like band-boxes) and stood on 'stilts' or 'spurs'. Traces of the latter can often be seen as three little scars on the base of the pots. Firing, however, resulted in pronounced crazing (crackling) of the glaze, associated with a brittle porous pot. This problem was never completely solved at the Fife Pottery. Ink stands (a popular line) were particularly vulnerable to staining by spilt ink. When J. K. MacKenzie was manager (1922–27) Wemyss was fired to 19 (1080°C) on Buller's rings – an expanding device that 'looked like a

Robert Methven Heron, c.1900.

Polo Mint'; peering through it permanently impared his eye-sight. Later he managed to increase the heat to 32–34 (1180–1190°C). After Sandland's arrival at the Pottery as chief decorator (1916), the powdered metallic oxide colours, bought in from Stoke, were mixed with oil, which enabled Wemyss to be fired at a somewhat higher temperature than before. The black ground of some of Sandland's plates has a characteristic tarry blackness. The last page of the 1920's Wemyss Ware price list offers 'Decorations on Black Ground, about 15% dearer than above List.' It also advertises 'Special Decorations to Order. Bedroom Ware, etc., quoted for, to match Wall Papers; and also in Apple Green and Pink Glazes, with monogram or Crest in White Enamel.' Enamelling would have required a third firing, and added to the cost.

21

## IV. WORKING CONDITIONS

By today's standards, life at the Fife Pottery was hard and poorly paid. Before the 48-hour week was introduced in the early 1920's, the potters worked a 60-hour, 6-day week. They started at 6 a.m., when Andrew Todd, the warehouseman, rang the bell at the works. They all lived near the Pottery, and at 9 a.m. knocked off for breakfast. They then worked till 6 p.m., with an hour off for lunch. Labourers were paid £1 a week, turners 30 shillings. There was no 'piece' work for the decorators: that would have lowered the standard of painting. Decorators were paid by the hour. Their top decorators, Karel Nekola and E. Sandland, both earned about £5 a week. J. K. MacKenzie, business manager after the First World War, counted and checked the pots at the end of the day.

To retain the brilliance of the colours so characteristic of Wemyss, a raw lead glaze was used. As this was a hazard to health, the workers had to be given, every morning, clean overalls and hot milk to avoid lead poisoning.

The Pottery, with its bell-tower and pan-tiled roofs, had an old-world appearance. In the summer evenings the potters often drifted back there to chat. They were an intelligent group of men, mostly Liberal and pro-Gladstone. Undated mugs inscribed 'Ye Tory and Ye Liberal Cock of Leith' refer to a candidate's political campaign across the Forth (Plate 81).

As previously stated, few written records survive from the Fife Pottery, but an evocative account of working life and processes in a Staffordshire Pottery (using methods very similar to those in use at the Fife Pottery) will be found in Arnold Bennett's powerful novel, *Anna of the Five Towns* (Chapter 8).

A group of Fife Pottery employees, c.1895

A group of Fife Pottery employees, c.1900.

# V. COMMERCIAL ASPECTS

In its Victorian heyday the sales of Wemyss Ware stood at around £800–£1,000 per month (in 1983 equivalent to c.£11,500 per month), with Thos. Goode & Co., South Audley Street, London SW1 the sole distributors. The ware was displayed in their Wemyss Room and proved very popular.

For a small Scottish Pottery, struggling in a highly competitive market, to launch a labour-intensive hand-painted ware was a considerable achievement. For instance, 10″ willow pattern plates from their general range were selling at 2/- (10 pence) per dozen, whilst a single bread-and-butter plate from the Wemyss range sold for 2/9 (14 pence). Miss Elizabeth Ritchie (later Mrs. Carl Nekola), who kept all the Fife Pottery's accounts from 1916–24, had quite a job sorting out the complexities of pricing.

The success of Wemyss Ware could not have come about without patronage, and Robert Heron was fortunate in receiving the interest and encouragement of the Wemyss family at Wemyss Castle. Lady Eva Wemyss and the Earl of Rosslyn were frequent visitors to the Pottery; indeed it was no doubt an interesting experience for visitors and not unprofitable for Heron. It was presumably largely due to the influence of the Wemyss family that the Fife Pottery was able to open up the upper class market for this relatively expensive ware.

To start with, Thos. Goode & Co. were agents for the whole of England. However, after the First World War the sale of Wemyss was much reduced, reaching a low output of around £120 per month. Goode's agency was then confined to the South of England and new agencies were accepted in other towns, including Liverpool, Newcastle, Chester and in Edinburgh.

Goode's reserved several Wemyss patterns and their records show these to have been as follows: Victoria (Double) and Princess (Single) Inkstands, Square honey box, Early morning tea-set (reserved in South of England only) and biscuit boxes and jam pots painted with roses and cherries. Details of these reserved patterns were included in a box of documents sent into the country at the beginning of the Second World War for safe-keeping. Efforts to trace the box have been unsuccessful.

The First World War, the General Strike of 1926, the Depression which followed it, together with minimum wage restrictions, inevitably had a disastrous effect on Wemyss production. It was accompanied by a change in aesthetic taste in the early 1920's. Wemyss never recovered from these compounded misfortunes.

An aerial view of the Fife Pottery in the 1920s. The Pottery House is to the top right of this photograph.

# VI. THE DECORATORS

*Karel Nekola* (b. 1857, d. 21 November 1915) was not only a talented under-glaze decorator, but a man with varied interests and ideas in advance of his time. It is therefore appropriate to give some account of his personality and interests as they have come down to us from J. K. MacKenzie (Jr.), Nekola's relatives in Kirkcaldy and limited publishing sources. There

Karel Nekola at work on an umbrella stand.

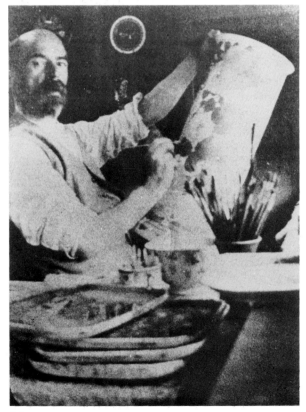

is no doubt that Nekola made a strong, almost legendary impression on the inhabitants of Gallatown.

Nekola had started life as a carpenter with his father in Bohemia, but after a serious fall he switched to decorating pottery. Apart from ceramics, Nekola was interested in the welfare and education of young people, and started the Boys' Club in Kirkcaldy. According to an appreciation in *The Fife Free Press* (4 December 1915), Nekola in his early years in Kirkcaldy 'was a drill instructor and teacher of gymnastics to the Boys' Institute in Hill Street. . . . Other bodies in which he took a keen interest were the Society of Free Gardeners and the Gallatown Young Men's Mutual Improvement Association, to the latter of which he was a tower of strength. The members valued most highly his contributions to their debates, since his opinions were so just and carefully thought out, and anticipated with unfeigned pleasure his essays on a wide variety of subjects.' Talks entitled 'Salt' and 'Coal' from less gifted members of the Association sound less inspiring. The same issue of *The Fife Free Press* goes on to tell us that 'in his early years of vigour and activity, Nekola was an untiring pedestrian, and there were few spots in the country within a radius of fifteen or twenty miles of the Lang Toon [Kirkcaldy] he did not explore'. He made water-colour sketches on these country walks, but those we have seen do not show the talents he displayed in the decoration of Wemyss Ware.

As time went on Nekola became increasingly crippled in his lower limbs, though his hands

seem to have been little affected. When the family moved to 7 Brandon Avenue, a small kiln was built for him at the bottom of the garden. Two girls carried down biscuit ware in a specially designed box, so that he could decorate and fire pots at home. Nekola's death certificate (1915) states that he died of Locomotor Ataxia – a paralytic lesion of the spinal cord (possibly a

A youthful Joe Nekola with his bike, c.1910.

24

wrong diagnosis). His gravestone is in Galla-town Churchyard.

We know much less about most of the other Wemyss decorators than we do about Karel Nekola. Taking them in approximate chronological order, they were as follows:

*David Grinton* was at the Pottery from c.1883–1922, throughout most of the Nekola period to the beginning of the Sandland period. He was almost a dwarf – about 4ft 6in. (an elderly informant's estimation of 2ft 6in. can be relegated to the Hobbits). On a visit to the Pountney Pottery near Bristol, one of us (P.H.D.) found his log book (dated 1907) showing that he did piece-work there – a procedure never adopted for Wemyss Ware at the Fife Pottery, because of the risk of lowering the standard of decoration. Grinton's characteristic signature in the log book (D. Grinton, neatly written in squared lower-case letters) has helped us to identify some of the pieces he decorated.

*John Brown* was one of the first decorators to be trained by Karel Nekola, being at the Fife Pottery in the 1880's and 1890's. He later moved to the Links Pottery (Methven's) where he was probably largely responsible for decorating Abbotsford Ware, the name being ink-stamped on the back. This was a near-copy of Wemyss Ware, the shapes being slightly different, the potting coarser, and the decoration of flowers and fruits usually rather stiff but effective. It might be added that more than one Wemyss decorator drifted away from the Fife Pottery from time to time, either because they got fed up, were given the push, or were perhaps offered a little more money. One of these may have been Sharp, who probably decorated an Abbotsford 2-handled mug with particularly splendid cocks and hens (Plate 7d).

The decorators in the painting shop were surrounded by examples of Wemyss painted by their colleagues. Under these circumstances it is only to be expected that a less experienced decorator would copy the work of another, and if only an impressed mark appears it will probably be impossible to identify the painter. The anonymous work of J. Brown may well be an example of what may be, for collectors, an unresolved dilemma.

*James Sharp* (b. c.1868, d. 1937) probably decorated Wemyss Ware from c.1883 to c.1919, staying on a little after Sandland's arrival. After Karel Nekola, Sharp was the best First Period decorator of Wemyss and was given many large pieces to paint; his manner of writing 'Wemyss' in lower case (almost copper-plate) is fortunately distinctive. Whether deserved or not, Sharp acquired a reputation for being 'taciturn'.

*Hugh McKinnon* (b. c.1870, d. 1943) we have no working dates for, but he was certainly at the Fife Pottery during much of the Nekola period. He apparently started before 1890 and had left by 1916.

*Christina (Teeny) McKinnon* (Hugh McKinnon's sister, b. 1884, d. c.1930) was a paintress, probably decorating Wemyss Ware from c.1898 to c.1925. Unfortunately we have been unable to distinguish between the work of Hugh and Christina McKinnon, though their combined output must have been prodigious. They decorated large numbers of small jam pots, plain or with modelled lids.

*James Adamson* had a sporadic decorating career at the Pottery, coming and going from

Eric Sandland, left, at the office door of the Fife Pottery, with two others.

the 1890's to 1920's. The work of he and John Brown is very seldom inscribed and therefore rarely attributable.

*Joseph (Joe) Nekola* joined the Fife Pottery as a Wemyss decorator in 1899, remaining there till 1910. He then set off to Buffalo in America for two years, returning to the Pottery in 1912. According to J. K. MacKenzie, Joe soon left to paint carts in Thornton, N. of Kirkcaldy, only returning to the Fife Pottery from 1928–30, after Sandland's death. He then moved to Bovey Tracey in Devon (see Chapter VIII).

*Carl Nekola* (Joe's brother, and usually spelt thus to distinguish him from his father Karel) was born on 18 December 1891. He was a Wemyss decorator at the Fife Pottery from 1919–24. We have been unable to identify his hand with any certainty from inscriptions on the base of the pots.

*Edwin Sandland* (b. 1873, d. 1928) was an important figure in the stylistic development of Wemyss Ware, decorating in the Fife Pottery from 1916–28. As his son informed us by letter, he was one of a line of Master potters going back several generations. His father owned the firm of Sandlands Ltd., Hanley, which produced decorated china in a Crown Derby style. Sandland was linked by marriage to Lucien Bullemeyer, the celebrated Minton decorator. Like Robert Heron, Sandland graduated through all the processes of production pottery.

He showed a preference for decorating (a field which he had studied at an Art College in Staffordshire) and eventually became a Director of the family firm. In 1915 Sandland (who played football for Stoke City) found himself out of harmony with the Pottery industry, joined the Army Pay Corps and was posted to Perth. Although Sandland had a placid temperament, he tended to worry overmuch. He was discharged from the Pay Corps for health reasons at the beginning of 1916, and was then engaged by Robert Heron & Son as chief decorator, thus replacing Karel Nekola who had died the year before. Sandland remained with the firm until his death in 1928, aged 54.

Coming to the Fife Pottery when the demand for Wemyss was in decline, Sandland did all he could to revive it. He was a remarkably rapid decorator, painting more than twice as many pots in a day as any of the previous painters – a feat that delighted the Management.

## VII. WEMYSS DECORATIONS

In this section Wemyss decoration is surveyed on a roughly progressional basis. Large pieces are mostly early, and belong to the Victorian-Edwardian era. Mainly for economic reasons and changes of taste, Wemyss pots got progressively smaller in the post-war period. In this chapter we recognise three phases – the Self-coloured, Karel Nekola and Sandland Periods. Information on markings and attribution is dealt with in Chapter X.

1. SELF-COLOURED PERIOD

We have retrieved eight crudely drawn duplicated sheets showing the rough shapes of 130 different pots (Page 47). Each of these sketches is captioned by a number on the sheets we have found. Nearly all these pieces were self-coloured Wemyss; most of the ones we have seen bear impressed numbers (but no names) that correspond to the drawings on the duplicated sheets. These numbers (cited in the next paragraph) are a different series to those used in the Wemyss Ware Price List of the early 1920's. This self-coloured ware was beautifully potted, of very fine finish and harder fired than most of the decorated ware that followed it. The glazes included crimson, orange, yellow, green, lilac and mazarine blue. We must assume that self-coloured Wemyss persisted successfully at least through much of the Nekola period, small pigs remaining particularly popular.

Fine examples of this early self-coloured phase include a huge orange Palm Pot (no. 90, 22 in. diam.), a very tall green vase (21·5 in., impressed Wemyss Ware, Fife Pottery), a two-handled gourd-like vase in crimson (47), a low crimson grooved pot reminiscent of an Ugli fruit (4), a Nairn Candlestick (96) and a wall plaque (22 in. diam., impressed Wemyss) bearing the impression of tree and fern leaves (cf. Plates 13–14). Two large vases shown on these duplicated sheets (23 and 24) bear embossed moulding and will be dealt with below. A set of grass-green plates have on their rims quotations from Robert Burns (Plate 10b).

## 2. KAREL NEKOLA PERIOD (c.1882–1915)

This was, without doubt, the finest period of Wemyss decoration and indeed the most fresh and boldly attractive product of the East Coast Potteries. Its success and prestige owe nearly everything to Robert Heron and his team of managers, potters, glazers and decorators, backed up by influential contacts and patrons. Although some decorations were much more popular than others, the firm painted almost anything they were asked for – even rhubarb and green peas (Plates 242 and 256)!

It is generally thought that most of the larger pieces of Wemyss were decorated during the Karel Nekola period. It therefore seems appropriate to deal with some of these first – 'Grand Wemyss' as the portrait painter, Derek Hill, has so aptly called it. We are here mainly emphasising particular decorators whose handiwork we have been able to identify with reasonable certainty. Naturally pride of place must be given to Karel Nekola, since he trained and guided the other decorators during this period. A very large, two-handled urn-shaped vase, heavily decorated with large pink convolvulus which the authors have seen, is clearly a very early Nekola piece.

A pair of Panel Vases (Plate 16), painted with mandarins standing beneath bamboos, is a piece of chinoiserie like nothing else in Wemyss Ware. No less exotic are the 'Chinese Garden Seats', one decorated with chrysanthemums and tropical butterflies, and another, probably slightly later one, with exotic birds, lilies and fanciful campanulas (Plates 20 and 18). Each

bears a Mediterranean shrub (*Smilax aspera*; *Vitex agnus-castus*) illustrated in Sibthorp and Smith's Flora Graeca. An Umbrella Stand (built in segments) is covered with Nekola's biggest cabbage roses, the base having a Greek key border (Plate 129). At Balmoral Castle there is a Tub Flower Pot (shaped like an ice-bucket) bearing a noble stag roaring at his rival. The famous Wemyss Fish – a 19-in. Carp with finely moulded scales – was copied from a much older Chinese Carp in Wemyss Castle.

A large Elgin vase (Plate 83b) has splendid cocks and hens swinging about on descending branches – a rather unexpected habitat. The smiling Fife Pottery cats go back to pre-Wemyss days, when they were decorated with bows and sparse gilt fur (Plate 32). The same shape persisted at least through the Wemyss period, being decorated with shamrock, dog roses, brown fur, etc. A yellow Wemyss cat (Plate 28) is painted with blue hearts and circles, being virtually a copy of the Gallé cats which Robert Heron probably saw in London or Paris. Three wise monkeys, sitting in and under a tree, decorate a Loving Cup (Plate 40). Wisteria hangs down a Rothes Flower Pot (Plate 174c), and a handsome Stanley Flower Pot (Plate 174a) is decorated with splendid crimson peonies – surely painted from life. Apparently from life, too, are a Grosvenor vase with pheasant's eye narcissus, the background painted light green to offset the white petals (Plate 194), and a Gordon Dessert Plate that bears a yellow iris with boldly twisted leaves (Plate 187c). Moulded Geese Flower Holders (Plates 113 and 114) were made

in three sizes; generally gaily painted, they resemble drakes rather than geese!

Pieces initialled by K. Nekola seem to be very rare, the practice not being officially allowed by the firm. One of these rarities is a particularly well-painted Comb Tray, with superlative cocks and hens, initialled 'KN' under glaze (Plate 76). A Heart Tray, with a dragonfly dive-bombing into reeds, can only have been painted by Nekola (Plate 75). Another Comb Tray shows a charming labour of love: a nuclear family of bears, two little ones dancing between their parents while father plays a melodeon (Plate 38). One of Nekola's most delightful pastoral pieces is one of the smallest – a Matchbox holder bearing a sheep and its lamb on one side, and a kid on the other (Plate 53). The smallest pieces are flowered hatpins and buttons (Plates 319–321). A most unusual series of five or six Gordon Dessert Plates depicts

Fife Pottery stationery with a note about John Huntbatch, a former employee.

different birds of prey (Plates 117–121). These plates are inscribed on the back with the name of the bird in French and Linnean Latin, and 'Karel Nekola'. They include an Eagle, Kestrel (1909), Black Kite and Long-eared Owl. A superbly painted Nekola plaque (1908) is decorated with a Hobby on a conifer. These bird plates, in style owing something to Audubon, were evidently copied from a French bird book we have been unable to trace. A ravishingly painted Comb Tray, with the name 'Violet Rosslyn' in a wreath of violets surmounted by a golden crown, is one of the finest pieces of Wemyss; an open book reading 'Le temps passe, L'amitié reste, 1897' conveniently dates it for us (Plate 262).

Bedroom sets were carefully decorated with ivy by Nekola and by Sharp. Flared and fluted Baskets with a 'rope handle' came in three sizes and were apparently popular throughout the Wemyss period, being decorated with a variety of flowers (Plates 154, 155 and 157).

As Karel Nekola was pre-eminent as a painter of cabbage roses, McKenzie told us how it was done. 'Nekola started with a twisting sweep of the brush, giving pink in the upper part of the rose, and a deeper shade below. White highlights were added. He then put in the leaves, the yellow veins last.'

After Heron's death in 1907 the check that was usually kept on Nekola's tendency to over-decorate was removed. From this time onwards examples of vases are prolifically covered with Nekola's cabbage roses from top to bottom, so that very little of the white body is visible (Plate 28

124). It is on plaques, however, that Nekola really let himself go, covering absolutely everything with decoration of a more laboured, often gloomy kind (Plate 270). His most successful plaque (Plate 266) is entirely filled by the displayed tail of a peacock – a present to Miss Williamson and now in the Huntly House Museum, Edinburgh.

A delightful (but now depleted) wash set is painted with stately flamingoes (Plate 115) and bears the monogram HP – probably one of the Rosebery family from Dalmeny Castle, whose family name was Primrose. A water-colour sketch of a tall flamingo jug has had the shape of its handle corrected in pencil – either by the Fife Pottery or by Thomas Goode & Co. (cf. Plate 343). The same HP cypher is found on water-colour sketches of ewers bearing pheasants, grouse and partridges – all painted and signed by K. Nekola but undated. These were evidently a special order.

Large vases aside, one might say that the broadly cylindrical shapes of Loving Cups, Mugs and Preserve jars are ideal for decoration. At the other extreme, narrow candlesticks (like the once popular Kintore (Plate 331) with its twisted stem and four fussy handles) present an obstacle to decoration. Candlesticks hark back to iron mediaeval or even Roman originals, cf. the Nairn Candlestick (Plate 14b). Of the almost two-dimensional shapes, Heart Trays (Plate 127), Comb Trays (Plate 237) and Gordon Dessert Plates (Plate 185) provide the most satisfactory base for bold decoration.

The sixtieth anniversary of Queen Victoria's

reign (1897) and the Coronations of Kings Edward VII (1902) and George V (1911) resulted in a spate of Commemorative cups and goblets (not in any Wemyss catalogue we have seen) carefully decorated with garlands of diminutive roses, shamrock, oak twigs, thistles and bay leaves (Plates 296 and 297). These impressive pieces are untypical of the usual Wemyss style, the painting being on a much smaller, detailed scale. Painted by Karel Nekola, they seem to have been a popular line, and are now much sought after by collectors.

In Edinburgh the city's Huntly House Museum has some splendid Wemyss of the Nekola period. This includes large Panel and 'Baluster' Vases (Plate 209), one painted with blue and brown arabesques, the other with exotic (even imaginary) flora. Beautiful wash sets (probably by K. Nekola) are decorated with wild ducks and dragonflies (Plates 69, 70 and 101).

Some particularly splendid Wemyss of the Nekola period is to be seen in the Kirkcaldy Museum. This includes a large Ewer and Basin decorated with boats (Fife yawls) sailing in the sunset (Plate 325), a Victoria Goblet painted with miraculous forget-me-nots and roses (Plate 281) and two gorgeous Baluster Vases. One of these (Plate 208) is painted with hydrangeas, oriental poppies and vetch, and is inscribed 'KN, 24.1.09, WEMYSS'. The other is decorated with delphiniums, irises, yellow geums, helichrysums (everlasting), shadowy grasses and a big bee. This vase, most surprisingly, is unmarked, and could lead to heady speculation as to its origin.

Was it decorated by Nekola to demonstrate his talents to Heron? Or even painted by Heron (a trained artist as well as a master potter) to show Nekola what he wanted Wemyss to be? A beautiful Loving Cup, garlanded with miniature yellow roses, commemorates the marriage of Lady Victoria Cavendish-Bentinck to Michael John Erskine Wemyss, 1918 (Plate 260).

Three Wemyss jugs, decorated during the Nekola period, deserve special mention. One is generally known as the 'Maid of Perth Jug' (Plate 322), and probably represents the Countess of Kinnoul at a pageant; it is built up in three horizontal sections. Another is the 'Beadle of Perth Jug' (Plate 323); the decoration is painted on a moulded jug that belongs to the Fife Pottery's general range; it has evidently been copied from a picture of George Fell (the town crier) in a book in Perth's City Library, dated 1906. The third is the tubby, jovial Sailor Jug (Plate 324). Some of the latter were apparently sent to Admiral Beatty. One Sailor Jug we have seen is initialled K. Nekola and dated 10 June 1910.

We must consider James Sharp (1890–c.1919) to have been the best decorator after his mentor, Karel Nekola. However, if a basal inscription is lacking, Sharp's work can be difficult to distinguish from Nekola's and sometimes even from Sandland's, unless we have Sharp's characteristic 'Wemyss' (almost copperplate) inscribed in lower case under glaze. The following are among some pieces that can be safely ascribed to Sharp: ewers and basins decorated with sweet peas – a subject at which he excelled; a fine pair of Elgin Vases (Plate 142) probably decorated to match a wallpaper; these bear fanciful pink bell-like flowers, pale pink and yellow roses, shadowy grasses, and bees with pointed abdomens. A small Teapot, delightfully painted with forget-me-nots and pink bows (Plate 183c), was part of Lady Victoria Wemyss' morning tea-set. Sharp decorated various Gordon Dessert plates, e.g. with violets, another decoration at which he excelled (Plate 189a). Gorse is a very rare pattern of Sharp's, and on a Chesham Fern Pot was evidently drawn from life (Plate 218b). One of his most beautiful pieces is a Mug with a strutting peacock (Plate 94). Sharp's dragonflies can be distinguished from those painted by Sandland: Sharp's are more carefully painted, and have pointed wings; those by Sandland usually have raggedly truncate wings. The Forbes family of Callender House in Falkirk had a large set of white broom (*Cytisus praecox*) decorated by Sharp. A remarkable Japan Vase, showing a dandelion in flower and fruit against a dark brown background, is an original and effective piece that may be Sharp's handiwork, or possibly Karel Nekola's (Plate 218a). Sharp's apples are often deeply umbilicate.

Although David Grinton was a decorator at the Fife Pottery from c.1883–1922, one seldom has a chance to identify his work with certainty. He did, however, decorate a large plaque of Gallatown Free Church, which bears his rather square-lettered 'D. Grinton'. The majority of his pieces remain unidentified. Adamson's work we cannot recognise with any certainty, but an Antique Candlestick, painted with undistinguished roses, bears the initial 'A' which may well be his (Page 48). The only piece of Wemyss we can identify with certainty as by John Brown is a stiff spray of apples on a plaque, impressed and inscribed 'Sinclairtown Established Church Bazaar, March 1906, J.B.'. In treatment it is extremely like an impressed Wemyss Heart Tray with apples and some of the rather stiffly decorated Abbotsford plaques.

Towards the end of the Nekola period we find an engaging, deliberately naïve series of pots often referred to as Earlshall Wemyss. Earlshall is an impressive sixteenth-century building near Leuchars in Fife, with a bestiary on the gallery ceiling. R. W. Mackenzie, a linen merchant, acquired the property in 1890 and had it restored by Robert Lorimer. Mackenzie was a colourful character who rode about in a Perth hat, brown riding coat, shepherd's plaid trousers and a tartan waistcoat (Plate 271). But here we must concentrate briefly on the pots that are associated with Earlshall, decorated in a diverse but distinctive style. Some rookery jugs, belonging to the Fife Pottery's general range, bear the legend 'Earlshall Faire, 1914' (Plate 275a); they were sold to raise money for the St. Michael's Golf Club near Leuchars. These, and various undated mugs, are painted with a rookery in the upper part, and often with rabbits beneath the trees. Although Canterbury Jugs are normally painted with Canterbury Bells, the Earlshall pieces (Plate 276b) are decorated with stylised topiary, sundials and peacocks (tail down) – themes derived from features in

Mackenzie's garden. A mug, quaintly painted in 1907 and inscribed 'Sanct Serf', belongs to this endearing series of pots (Plate 279); it bears tiny cut-out trees and toy-like yellow-and-brown birds. We must add that rookery wash sets became popular in Fife (Plate 274), many of them later too hastily painted by Sandland. Irish linen towels, made by Ross of Belfast, accompanied the rookery bedroom ware (Plate 275d).

Karel Nekola may well have decorated the Heart Trays with Bryant & May match-boxes and curling tongs being heated in a methylated flame (Plate 330). Decorated mottoes and proverbs on pin trays, etc. were a popular line in the Edwardian period: for example, on a Pin Tray are the words 'I look for something sweet to send to you, and the violets asked if they would do' (Plate 318e); a morning teapot, decorated with a crowing cock and the rising sun, reads 'Many are called but few rise early' (Plate 312b). A Cigar-Holder and Ash Tray, painted with a glowing cigar, comments that 'Life is but a short smoke' – a premonition of the dangers of tobacco? (Plate 312a).

Joseph Nekola was a prolific decorator, but pieces which do not bear his inscription (neat lower case 'wemyss' followed by a full stop) are often difficult to distinguish from some other decorators' work. He spent a year or two in Canada, and sent home as presents two signed plates dated 1912: one of a red squirrel on a larch bough, the other of an orchid spray (Odontoglossum) with a green jungly background. Joe was an enthusiastic painter of cabbage roses, but these have fewer petals and less highlights than his father's blooms. Often well executed on Baskets and Squat Teapots, they can become rather monotonous. Joe also painted a pleasing series of fruit plates: apples, cherries, strawberries and plums.

Before we pass on to decoration in the Sandland Period, attention should be drawn to the care that was given to the 'trimming' on Wemyss pots, especially during the Nekola phase. The upper or lower edges of the pots are often defined by a band or swagged border. There is a tendency for the band, in later pieces, to be reduced almost to a line, and for crimson bands to be superseded by bluish-green ones. In contrast, blue-green swagged borders define the upper edge of many pieces. With jam pots and the larger preserve jars, both the top of the receptacle and the edge of the lid have matching swagged borders, giving a most pleasing effect (Plate 239). However, this procedure was not consistently followed. It is clear that great care was given to see that the borders harmonised with the main decoration on the pot, so that an overall unity prevailed. This is particularly evident on Mugs and Loving Cups. Careful attention was given to the decoration of the handles of Wemyss Ware. Variations of the palmette decoration are often very successful on handles of Ewers and at the base of some other larger pieces, e.g. Umbrella Stands and Bute Vases (Plate 135a).

It seems relevant here to mention the use of pounces – a technique adopted by some of the less gifted Wemyss decorators. Pounces were pieces of paper bearing the perforated outline of (for instance) cocks and hens. The decorator applied the pounce to the pot at the biscuit stage, brushing charcoal over the paper so that a row of black dots was faintly stencilled on the pot. This procedure enabled the painter to decorate more quickly and accurately, but could result in a somewhat mechanical product. A decorator of Karel Nekola's calibre needed no such aid. The same method was used in the decoration of Cat-and-Dog ware at the Pountney Pottery near Bristol.

## 3. SANDLAND PERIOD (1916–28)

Edwin Sandland continued the decorative traditions of the Nekola Period, but also branched out into a distinctive style of his own. It should be remembered that casting techniques were probably not introduced at the Fife Pottery till shortly after the Great War (c.1920) and are therefore confined to the Sandland period. We have already referred to the rapidity of Sandland's free-style decorating. His Chrysanthemums, for instance, were particularly free and prolific, in pink, violet and yellow (Plate 181); so were the pink dog roses at which he excelled (see Combe Flower Pot, Plate 150b). He also painted dog roses in oil paint on bone china tea-sets bought in from Copeland.

Were it not for the late introduction of casting, and the style in which Sandland wrote 'Wemyss' on the bottom of his pots, we would often find it difficult to distinguish many of his more traditional pieces from those by K. Nekola or Sharp. Sandland's oranges, with their stippled, pore-like surface, were evidently one of his favourite decorations (Plate 250); a delightful Lemon Squeezer was given similar treatment (Plate 235b). A probably unique, modelled oblong box (uncatalogued) was boldly decorated, apparently by Sandland, with a branch of thickly painted green figs (Plate 235a). He was almost certainly the decorator of a splendid ewer and basin cunningly painted with Arum lilies, so that the white spathes contrast with the dark green foliage embracing the ewer (Plate 198).

Sandland's most striking innovation was the painting of pots with a black background. This was particularly effective on a Gordon Dessert Service, where it formed a tar-like 'canvas' for various luscious fruits; the white rim of these plates has a falsely perforate black-and-white border (Plate 230). Sandland also decorated a most original large bowl with white roses on a partly black ground. A striking Sandland bowl (signed ES) is covered all over with dog roses on a multicoloured, predominantly blue background (Plate 150c). It recalls those glass bowls that Edwardian children covered with a mosaic of coloured silver paper. An exceptionally large Lady Eva Vase, painted with pink dog roses, has a striking band of white roses on a black central band; this is a late, cast piece (Plate 150a). One of his finest pieces is a large Japan Vase with stately daffodils, the flowers positioned on a broad black band near the top (Plate 164a).

A late innovation seems to have been the New Honey Jar (Plate 67b), its conical lid being like a tall skep, bearing a knop or bee on the top. Low, cast jam pots were a delightful line at this period, the lids bearing modelled and painted leaves, fruits and flowers (Plate 241). These pots were mostly decorated by Hugh and Teeny McKinnon and by D. Grinton. It seems that the prototype of this delightful, good-selling line was either Wedgwood & Co. of Tunstall (the name being impressed beneath the lid), or another version by C. Perret Gentil of Mentone Pottery (France). The latter is inscribed on the base 'P.G.M.' and bears a slender dragon-fly mark.

In the 1920's it became increasingly difficult to sell Wemyss. The introduction of a minimum wage had a serious effect on all Potteries in Scotland. But there were also other reasons for decline. Cabbage roses, ribbons and bows went out of fashion after the War. The installation of bathrooms, central heating and electric light struck a blow to wash sets and candlesticks. Fountain pens proved more convenient than inkstands. Sandland made some brave attempts at new styles, including the Leven Vase, tall and tapering (thrown) with bold blue Irises, and a cast columnar vase decorated with black sailing boats. He also produced a 3-handled mug with galleons in full sail – an unexpected apparition on the Firth of Forth.

Sandland was evidently responsible for Langtoun Ware, which bore on its base a printed circular cartouche topped by a thistle. This line can be taken as a parting shot in the direction of Art Deco. A Langtoun biscuit barrel sports a stylised design of bananas and cherries, and various pieces painted with a bold floral pattern outlined with black (inscribed W66). We have seen a 'Jazzy Wemyss'* Quaich painted by Sandland, but most of this garish polychrome ware was decorated by Joseph Nekola on his return to the Fife Pottery in 1928 as the last Wemyss decorator. It was the end of the road for the Fife Pottery. Unsold Wemyss littered the works. On 30 May 1930 an advertised sale was held to dispose of the stock that remained. To avoid confusion it should be understood that some of the biscuit ware (impressed 'Wemyss') was taken away by studio potters who painted it in their own manner, often putting their initials on the base.

---

* An apt term coined by Lady Anstruther, previously an antique dealer in Edinburgh. Like most Wemyss, 'Jazzy Wemyss' looks its best on mahogany or against plain coloured walls.

# VIII. BOVEY TRACEY PERIOD AND WEMYSS-LIKE WARES

After the closure of the Fife Pottery, Joe Nekola decorated an interesting plate showing three different fruits (inscribed Wemyss, Trial) which he sent to the Bovey Pottery Co. in Devon (Plate 257). This approach was successful. He moved to Bovey Tracey the same year (1930), taking many of the Fife moulds with him, and continued to perpetuate what he called 'the spirit of Wemyss'. It may seem surprising that a small pottery in Devon was able to produce and sell Wemyss roses etc. fairly successfully after the style had petered out in Fife. This was presumably made possible by the strong Art Pottery

Kilns at the Bovey Pottery in Devon.

tradition in Devon and Cornwall which provided an ambiance sympathetic to colourful hand-painted ware. The pots were harder fired at Bovey Tracey than in Fife, so that crazing of the glaze virtually stopped. They are usually inscribed 'Wemyss, made in England', 'J.N.' or, in the case of the larger, better pieces, 'Nekola pinxt'. However, although the ware was less easily broken, it often acquired a somewhat greasy or pigskin finish which we find less attractive than the Fife Pottery product. In the 1930's a Czech, Jan Plichta, became sole agent. A series of new moulds was produced, including some sentimental animals (nodding cats and tiny elephants, etc.) which the unfortunate Joe was compelled to paint to survive; they bore Plichta's stamp. Joe Nekola died of diabetes in 1952. When the Bovey Pottery closed in 1957, the rights to Wemyss Ware were acquired by Royal Doulton.

We can hardly end this chapter without dealing briefly with some Wemyss copies. One of them was Abbotsford Ware, a name applied to two different wares apparently made by David Methven & Son, Kirkcaldy. The first of these was a *self-coloured* ware very similar to self-coloured Wemyss, but back-stamped 'Abbotsford'. This was presumably more or less contemporary with early self-coloured Wemyss, both lines bearing different impressed serial numbers and probably produced in competition with one another in the early 1880's, before the appearance of decorated Wemyss in 1883.

The second, *decorated* Abbotsford Ware bears

Bovey Tracey days – Joe Nekola, Esther Weekes and others.

a rather close resemblance to decorated Wemyss and was presumably in competition with it. We are not sure when it was made, but it seems reasonable to suggest (on economic grounds) that it was produced between Heron's death (1906) and the 1914–18 War. Decorated Abbotsford is more coarsely potted than Wemyss Ware, the shapes being slightly different and the decoration often stiffer. We have been told that much of it (including fruits on concave plaques) was probably decorated by John Brown (one of the Wemyss decorators), but a few pieces are more finely painted and may be the handiwork of Sharp, who is said to have decorated at Methven's Pottery for a while. Decorators from both Potteries drifted away (and back) from time to time, Karel Nekola being a rare example of stability.

It should be added here that other marked, more simply decorated lines were produced by

Methven's Pottery: Auld Heather, Airlie and Nisbet Wares, the painting usually incorporating a slender version of Methven's 'Maggie Rooney' rose pattern with simple blue and green brush decoration.

Apart from decorated Abbotsford Ware, there were other imitators of Wemyss Ware outside Scotland. Perhaps the best exponent of the *genre* was a decorator in the Llanelly Pottery in S.W. Wales, named Arthur Shufflebotham (Shuff for short). 'He is said to have abandoned his wife and children and left Fishponds in Bristol for Llanelly Pottery about the year 1908. He was a heavy drinker and before starting work would regularly consume four glasses of rum in the Golden Lion outside the gates of the Pottery . . . He painted many patterns, but the wild rose, tea rose and various fruits and flowers were the most common . . . All pieces marked Llanelly or Llanelly Pottery are his work since he was the only person permitted to use these marks. Arthur Shufflebotham worked at the Pottery until sometime during the First World War (probably about 1915), when he left, somewhat unexpectedly, and nothing more was heard of him.' (Extract from Dilys Jenkins, *Llanelly Pottery*, 1968.) It seems likely that Shuff came from the Pountney Pottery, Fishponds, Bristol, where elegantly cast cock-and-hen pottery was being stylishly decorated by George Stewart (signed G.S.). About this time two other Wemyss-style wares (both marked) deserve special mention, both for their elegant shapes and decoration. One was marked Ye Olde English (S. F. & C. England) and is Edwardian in style. A more serious Continental competitor was the famous firm of Villeroy and Boch, Dresden, which produced well-shaped pottery tea ware. The paint was apparently sprayed on through a masking device. All records of this firm were destroyed in the bombing of Dresden during the Second World War. Roses and cherries were the commonest decorations on both wares.

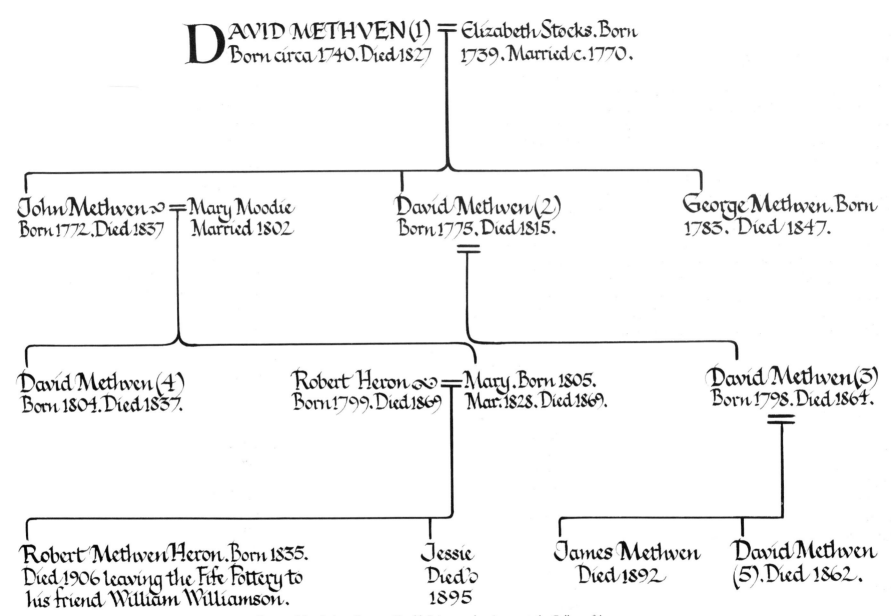

**DAVID METHVEN (1)** Born circa 1740. Died 1827 ⚯ Elizabeth Stocks. Born 1739. Married c. 1770.

John Methven ⚯ Mary Moodie
Born 1772. Died 1837 Married 1802

David Methven (2)
Born 1775. Died 1815.

George Methven. Born 1783. Died 1847.

David Methven (4)
Born 1804. Died 1837.

Robert Heron ⚯ Mary. Born 1805.
Born 1799. Died 1869 Mar. 1828. Died 1869.

David Methven (3)
Born 1798. Died 1864.

Robert Methven Heron. Born 1835.
Died 1906 leaving the Fife Pottery to
his friend William Williamson.

Jessie
Died
1895

James Methven
Died 1892

David Methven
(5). Died 1862.

Engrossed by Robert Parsons, Herald Painter and scrivener at the College of Arms.

34

# IX. LIST OF WEMYSS DECORATIONS

Although a great diversity of Wemyss decoration is displayed in this book, it may be of interest and of use to collectors to group the different types of decoration under six headings: Mammals (including Man), Birds, Fish, Insects, Flowers and Plants, and Designs, patterns and objects. A complication, however, occurs in regard to chimeras that we find on some large Wemyss vases – i.e. the apparent grafting of one genus onto another! This probably arose by copying (or adapting) designs from wallpapers which are advertised in the *Wemyss Ware Catalogue* of the 1920's, p. 7. Even a few of the disparate parts of chimeras are beyond identification. No doubt other decorations will be found.

## MAMMALS (including Man)
'Beadle of Perth'
Beagle
Bears
Boar's Head
Bulls
Bulldog
Cats
Chamois
Cherub
Cow
Deer
Dog
Dolphin
Dragons
Fox (incised)
Frog Mug
Goat
Hares
Heads of Two Girls
Highland Cattle
Horse and Hound
Kittens
Lamb
Lion (incised)
Mandarins
'Maid of Perth'
Monkeys
Pigs:
    apples
    black and white
    blue
    flambe
    four-leaf clover
    green
    mauve
    'Paddy'
    pig in stye
    pink
    shamrock
    thistle
    white
    yellow
Pony
Rabbits
Sailor
Sheep
Smoker
Squirrel
Stag
Woman and Child

## BIRDS
Birds of Prey:
    Black Kite
    Eagle
    Hobby
    Honey Buzzard
    Kestrel
    Long-eared Owl
Bullfinch
Canary in cage
Cocks: black, brown
Duck: mallard and drake
Exotic blue and yellow birds
Flamingoes
Geese
Goldfinch
Grouse
Hen: black, brown
Heron
Owl
Peacock
Pheasant
Robin
Rooks
Sand Martin
Sparrow
Swallow
Swan
Turkey

FISH and REPTILES
Carp
Char
Dogfish
Goldfish
Lizard
Salmon

INSECTS
Bee
Beetle
Butterflies:
    Peacock
    Red Admiral
    Tropical
Caterpillar
Dragonfly
Fly
Grasshopper
Ladybird

FLOWERS and PLANTS
Anemones
Apple Blossom
Arum Lilies
Aster
Auricula
Bamboo
Bay Leaves (wreaths)
Bindweed/Convolvulus
Bramble
Buttercup
Campanula
Campion

36

Canterbury Bells
Carnation
Celandine
Chrysanthemum (pink, white, yellow)
Cineraria
Clover (red)
Convolvulus (pink, white, yellow, blue)
Corn
Corn Marigold
Corncockle
Cornflower
Crocus (yellow, purple)
Crown Imperial
Daffodil (trumpet)
Daisies (lawn and various)
Dandelion
Delphinium
Dead Nettle, Spotted
Dicentra spectabilis
Elm branch in bud
Exotic Flowers
Ferns:
    Bracken
    Dryopteris
    Maidenhair
        Spleenwort
Forget-me-not
Foxglove
Fritillary
Fuchsia
Geum
Gorse
Grasses
Heather (Ling)
Helichrysum (Everlasting)

Holly
Honeysuckle
Hoya carnosa
Hyacinth
Hydrangea
Iris
Ivy
Kingcup
Laburnum
Larch cones
Large Birdsfoot Trefoil
Laurel
Lilac
Lilies
Lily of the valley
Marguerite
Marsh Marigold
Mimosa
Morning glory
Narcissus (pheasant's eye, etc.)
Nasturtium (red, yellow)
Oak Leaves
Orange Blossom
Ox-eye daisy
Palm
Pansies
Passion flower
Pelargonium
Paeony
Persimon
Poppies (oriental and hybrids)
Prunus
Pyrethrum
Red Campion
Reeds

Rhubarb
Rose buds
Rosemary
Roses (Cabbage): red, yellow, white
Roses (Dog): pink, white
Shamrock
Smilax aspera
Snowdrops
Sunflower
Sweet Peas
Thistle
Thistle-shaped vase
Topiary
Trees and bushes (sponged)
Trefoil (Bird's foot)
Tulips (red; Parrot)
Vetch (Common)
Vine leaves
Violets
Vitex agnus-castus
Water Lilies (yellow)
White Broom (Cytisus praecox)
Wisteria
Wych elm in bud
 Yellow Vetchling (Lathyrus aphaca)

FRUITS etc
Acorns
Apple
Blackberry/
    bramble
Cherries
Currants red, black
Damson
Fig

Filbert
    (Corylus maxima)
Gooseberries green, red
Grapes purple, green
Greengage
Hazel nuts
Holly berries
Lemon
Orange
Peach?
Pear
Peas
Persimmon?
Plum
Raspberry
Rhubarb
Strawberry

DESIGNS, PATTERNS and OBJECTS
Arabesques
Arm Chair
Art Nouveau (after Mackintosh)
Arrow
Basket
Black crazing
Boats
Bows
Bridge
Cage
Candle
Church
Cigar
Cockles
Crests
Crown
Curling Tongs

Curtains
Dysart with St. Serfs church tower
Enamelling
Flags
Fur
Galleons
Garden Tools
Greek key border
Green stripes
Hearts
Hives
Imari pattern
Lanyard
Melodeon
Monograms
Mottling: dark blue on red
Mottoes
Nests
Palmette decorations
Randolph Wemyss Memorial Hospital
Ribbons
Road
Scrolls
Sea
Skull
Snow scene
Stars
Sun
Sunset
Town Hall Clock
Turkey Pattern (brown and blue)
Water
Waves
Wemyss Castle
Windmill

# X. MARKINGS

Wemyss Ware was nearly always marked and, apart from covers and the occasional cup, unmarked pots are indeed rarities. Almost always, when one is offered an unmarked piece it turns out to be, on close examination, Abbotsford or similar ware from other potteries.

Wemyss was marked from its inception, early pieces being marked with the name of the firm (Robert Heron, Fife Pottery Kirkcaldy NB). An impressed semicircular backstamp with Wemyss Wares, R.H. & S. (characteristic of the K. Nekola period) was often used, as were straight backstamps in varying sizes with the word WEMYSS. Goode's underglaze oval inked backstamp was considered a mark of approval, but was applied at the Fife Pottery, not in London.

When a pot had a turned base the turner applied the backstamp by hand, leaving a clean impression which required no amplification (i.e. Mugs have turned bases and are rarely found with painted marks). Where the backstamp was incorporated into the mould the impression would gradually get clogged by use and the decorator would often supplement poorly impressed marks with a painted mark. When Wemyss is inscribed this was always done by the decorator, using the last colour on his brush.

As each individual had his own style, it is possible to identify the work of several decorators by their painted marks. However, as this style changed gradually over the years, it should be clearly understood that the inscriptions illustrated here serve as the 'signatures' of those decorators at a specific period. For instance the mark on Page 40(9) is that of Karel Nekola towards the end of his working life. A Nekola's earlier inscription was bolder and more stylish. (Page 39(3b).) Inscriptions were also affected by the angle and speed at which they were written, so that one cannot always be certain of the attribution. The only inscriptions we can usually be sure about are those of Karel Nekola, Sharp, Grinton, Joe Nekola and Sandland. Others remain anonymous.

1. Semi-circular impressed mark on base of Mug. Probably one of the earlier backstamps.

2. The Earlshall design, introduced in 1914, has a painted 'Earlshall' mark often accompanied by an impressed 'Wemyss' mark.

3a. Typical painted mark by Sandland.

4. Impressed 'Wemyss'. This piece also carries the mark of the London agents Thomas Goode & Co.

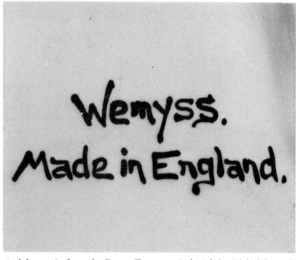

6. A large pig from the Bovey Tracey period with Joe Nekola's neatly painted mark. Note that Joe Nekola often ended the word with a full stop, and decorated the last S with a serif.

3b. Possibly early mark by Karel Nekola.

5. A generously marked plate. The earlier semi-circular backstamp is supported by a painted mark by an illusive decorator and the official cartouche of the London agent Thomas Goode & Co.

7. A Wemyss backstamp with the cartouche of the London agent.

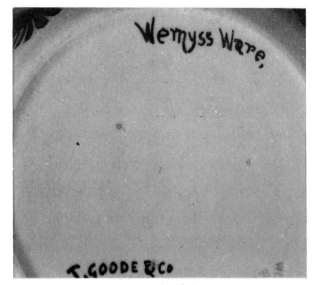

10. Three clear marks. Impression, cartouche and inscription.

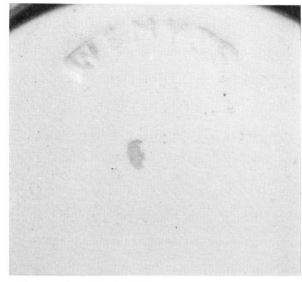

12. An unusual semi-circular backstamp.

8. A well marked saucer. Artist unidentified.

9. The impressed mark, lost in the footrim, is supported by the inscription of the master, Karel Nekola.

11. A distinctive inscription; artist unknown.

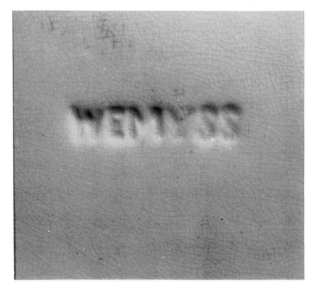

13. A large backstamp, used for bigger pots.

14. This inscription could be Joe Nekola's.

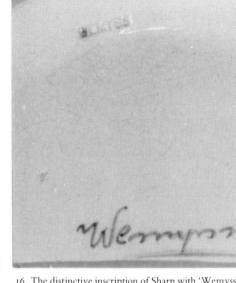

16. The distinctive inscription of Sharp with 'Wemyss' impressed.

18. A 'special' signed by Karel Nekola and dated 22nd October 1909. This pot, painted for a young lady named 'Rosemary', is decorated with sprigs of rosemary.

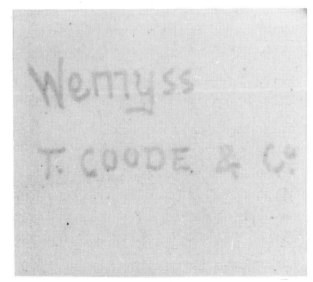

15. The inscription could be David Grinton's.

17. Inscription by an unidentified decorator.

19. A circular mark.

20. A late cartouche dating from c.1926. A similar cartouche was used for 'Langtoun Ware' which was introduced around the mid 1920's.

# XI. NOTES ON PRICE LISTS AND CATALOGUES

The firm of Robert Heron & Son produced at least five price lists between 1855 and 1930 but only one of these, the first, is accurately dated. None of the others has been found complete, that is the price list together with the accompanying photographs for identifying shapes. The price lists can be summarised as follows:

1) Price list of general range wares dated 1855. This list was still in use until the end of the 1914–18 War. (Shown opposite.)

2) Duplicated sheets showing 130 numbered shapes which presumably accompanied a price list. These pots were probably those produced in self-coloured glazes; in our opinion the sheets date from c.1880. The numbers on the sheets correspond with the numbers impressed into various early pots which we have seen. (Page 47.)

3) A photograph dated from c.1890, showing pots numbered 98 to 126. The price list and the other photographs which accompanied it have so far not been traced. (Page 47.)

4) A price list dated from the early 1920's and probably issued at the beginning of that decade together with two sheets of photographs showing pots numbered 1 to 68. (See (Pages 43–47.)

5) A price list dated from the 1920's and possibly dating from c.1927. The photographs matching this price list have not been seen by us. (Page 51.)

42

Price list, dated March 1855, showing the wares produced by Robert Heron & Son, before Wemyss was thought of!

The numbering sequence used in the c.1890 price list was followed in the subsequent editions and we thus have three photographs from the set of five which accompanied these lists. It is from these that we have been able to identify the pots by their proper names as used by the Fife Pottery. Former employees have helped us to identify various items listed in the price lists and for which the appropriate photograph was missing.

When preparing the price lists the pottery staff appear to have arranged the pots in five groups for the photographer and then numbered the items in the sequence in which they were thus arranged. The result is a mixture of pots in no special order but with occasional duplication and some omissions (i.e. item 12 includes dog bowls and an egg cup which was probably missed in the numbering sequence). The inconsistencies are sorted out on page 44.

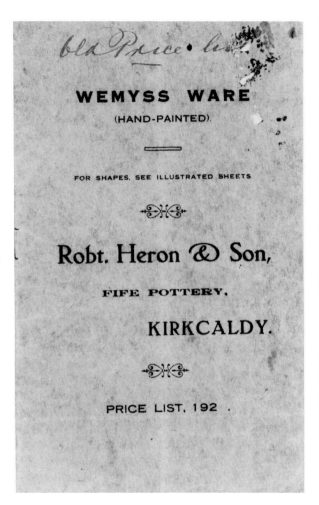

a, b, c, d. The Fife Pottery catalogue issued c.1920.

Japan vases receive three separate entries (numbers 4, 82 and 104).

Beaker vases appear under numbers 38 and 39 and under a change of name (brush vase) at entry 123.

Mugs with one, two or three handles are listed under number 23 and also at 108.

Gordon Dessert plates appear as number 24 and again (as dessert ware) at 177.

Some shapes appear, with minor modification, under a different name. Number 21 – a Frilled Bowl – reappears as an Epsom Basket at entry 15, the modification being, in this case, the addition of a basket-work handle.

Quaichs cause confusion, being listed five times and with four quite different shapes:

No. 10 Tall Quaich, large (Plates 282 and 283).
No. 60 Tall Quaich, small (Plate 33e).
No. 57 Low Quaich Dessert Dish, small (Plate 254b).
Low Quaich Dessert Dish, large (Plate 67).
No. 95 Quaich preserve dish.

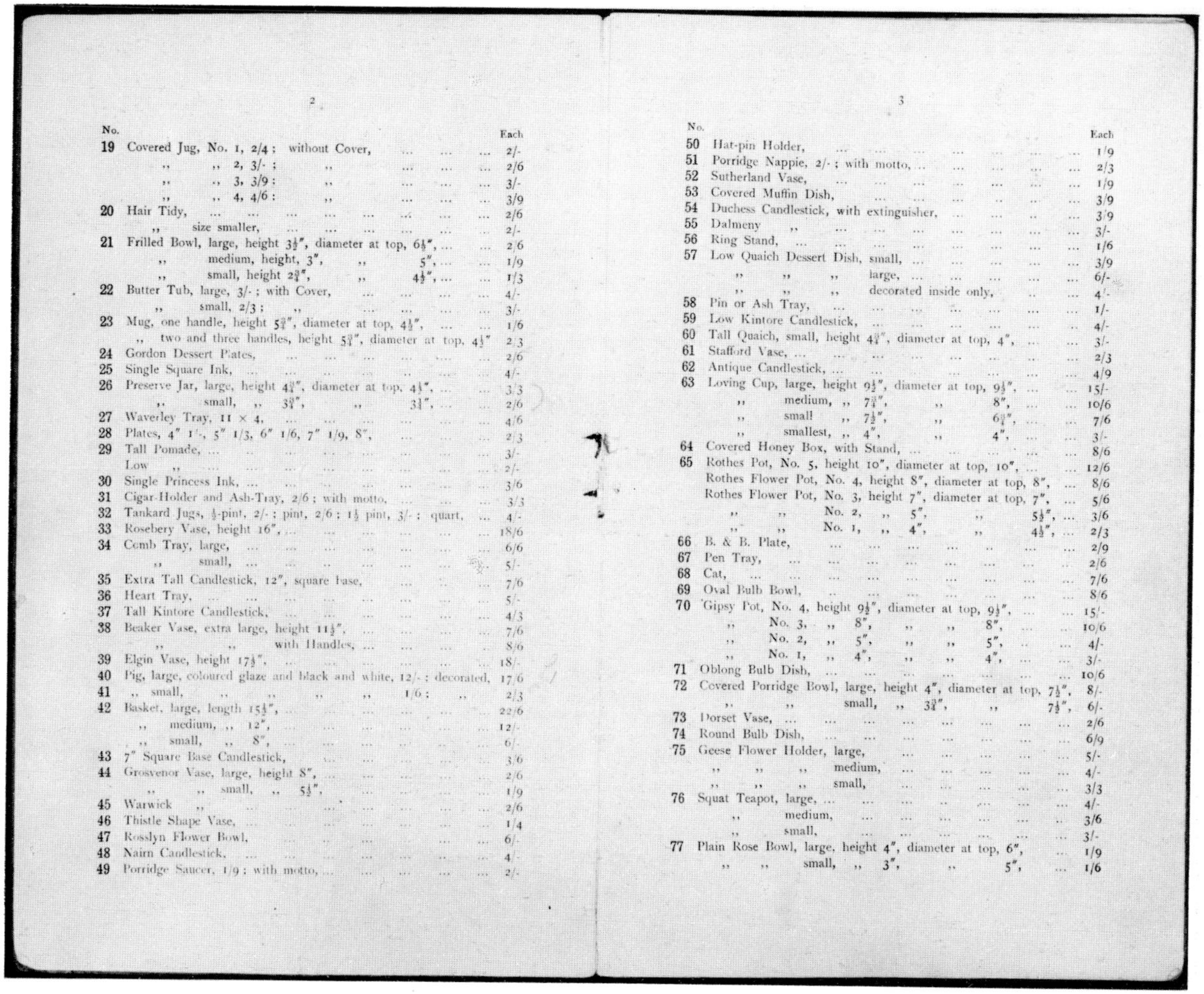

2

| No. | | Each |
|---|---|---|
| 19 | Covered Jug, No. 1, 2/4 ; without Cover, | 2/- |
| | ,, ,, 2, 3/- ; ,, | 2/6 |
| | ,, ,, 3, 3/9 : ,, | 3/- |
| | ,, ,, 4, 4/6 : ,, | 3/9 |
| 20 | Hair Tidy, | 2/6 |
| | ,, size smaller, | 2/- |
| 21 | Frilled Bowl, large, height 3½", diameter at top, 6½", | 2/6 |
| | ,, medium, height, 3", ,, 5", | 1/9 |
| | ,, small, height 2¾", ,, 4½", | 1/3 |
| 22 | Butter Tub, large, 3/- ; with Cover, | 4/- |
| | ,, small, 2/3 ; ,, | 3/- |
| 23 | Mug, one handle, height 5¾", diameter at top, 4½", | 1/6 |
| | ,, two and three handles, height 5¾", diameter at top, 4½" | 2/3 |
| 24 | Gordon Dessert Plates, | 2/6 |
| 25 | Single Square Ink, | 4/- |
| 26 | Preserve Jar, large, height 4¾", diameter at top, 4¼", | 3/3 |
| | ,, small, ,, 3¾", ,, 3¼", | 2/6 |
| 27 | Waverley Tray, 11 × 4, | 4/6 |
| 28 | Plates, 4" 1/-, 5" 1/3, 6" 1/6, 7" 1/9, 8", | 2/3 |
| 29 | Tall Pomade, | 3/- |
| | Low ,, | 2/- |
| 30 | Single Princess Ink, | 3/6 |
| 31 | Cigar-Holder and Ash-Tray, 2/6 ; with motto, | 3/3 |
| 32 | Tankard Jugs, ½-pint, 2/- ; pint, 2/6 ; 1½ pint, 3/- ; quart, | 4/- |
| 33 | Rosebery Vase, height 16", | 18/6 |
| 34 | Comb Tray, large, | 6/6 |
| | ,, small, | 5/- |
| 35 | Extra Tall Candlestick, 12", square base, | 7/6 |
| 36 | Heart Tray, | 5/- |
| 37 | Tall Kintore Candlestick, | 4/3 |
| 38 | Beaker Vase, extra large, height 11½", | 7/6 |
| | ,, ,, with Handles, | 8/6 |
| 39 | Elgin Vase, height 17½", | 18/- |
| 40 | Pig, large, coloured glaze and black and white, 12/- ; decorated, | 17/6 |
| 41 | ,, small, ,, ,, ,, ,, 1/6 ; ,, | 2/3 |
| 42 | Basket, large, length 15½", | 22/6 |
| | ,, medium, ,, 12", | 12/- |
| | ,, small, ,, 8", | 6/- |
| 43 | 7" Square Base Candlestick, | 3/6 |
| 44 | Grosvenor Vase, large, height 8", | 2/6 |
| | ,, ,, small, ,, 5½", | 1/9 |
| 45 | Warwick ,, | 2/6 |
| 46 | Thistle Shape Vase, | 1/4 |
| 47 | Rosslyn Flower Bowl, | 6/- |
| 48 | Nairn Candlestick, | 4/- |
| 49 | Porridge Saucer, 1/9 ; with motto, | 2/- |

3

| No. | | Each |
|---|---|---|
| 50 | Hat-pin Holder, | 1/9 |
| 51 | Porridge Nappie, 2/- ; with motto, | 2/3 |
| 52 | Sutherland Vase, | 1/9 |
| 53 | Covered Muffin Dish, | 3/9 |
| 54 | Duchess Candlestick, with extinguisher, | 3/9 |
| 55 | Dalmeny ,, | 3/- |
| 56 | Ring Stand, | 1/6 |
| 57 | Low Quaich Dessert Dish, small, | 3/9 |
| | ,, ,, ,, large, | 6/- |
| | ,, ,, ,, decorated inside only, | 4/- |
| 58 | Pin or Ash Tray, | 1/- |
| 59 | Low Kintore Candlestick, | 4/- |
| 60 | Tall Quaich, small, height 4¾", diameter at top, 4", | 3/- |
| 61 | Stafford Vase, | 2/3 |
| 62 | Antique Candlestick, | 4/9 |
| 63 | Loving Cup, large, height 9½", diameter at top, 9½", | 15/- |
| | ,, medium, ,, 7¾", ,, 8", | 10/6 |
| | ,, small ,, 7½", ,, 6¾", | 7/6 |
| | ,, smallest, ,, 4", ,, 4", | 3/- |
| 64 | Covered Honey Box, with Stand, | 8/6 |
| 65 | Rothes Pot, No. 5, height 10", diameter at top, 10", | 12/6 |
| | Rothes Flower Pot, No. 4, height 8", diameter at top, 8", | 8/6 |
| | Rothes Flower Pot, No. 3, height 7", diameter at top, 7", | 5/6 |
| | ,, ,, No. 2, ,, 5", ,, 5½", | 3/6 |
| | ,, ,, No. 1, ,, 4", ,, 4½", | 2/3 |
| 66 | B. & B. Plate, | 2/9 |
| 67 | Pen Tray, | 2/6 |
| 68 | Cat, | 7/6 |
| 69 | Oval Bulb Bowl, | 8/6 |
| 70 | Gipsy Pot, No. 4, height 9½", diameter at top, 9½", | 15/- |
| | ,, No. 3, ,, 8", ,, ,, 8", | 10/6 |
| | ,, No. 2, ,, 5", ,, ,, 5", | 4/- |
| | ,, No. 1, ,, 4", ,, ,, 4", | 3/- |
| 71 | Oblong Bulb Dish, | 10/6 |
| 72 | Covered Porridge Bowl, large, height 4", diameter at top, 7½", | 8/- |
| | ,, ,, small, ,, 3¾", ,, 7½", | 6/- |
| 73 | Dorset Vase, | 2/6 |
| 74 | Round Bulb Dish, | 6/9 |
| 75 | Geese Flower Holder, large, | 5/- |
| | ,, ,, ,, medium, | 4/- |
| | ,, ,, ,, small, | 3/3 |
| 76 | Squat Teapot, large, | 4/- |
| | ,, medium, | 3/6 |
| | ,, small, | 3/- |
| 77 | Plain Rose Bowl, large, height 4", diameter at top, 6", | 1/9 |
| | ,, ,, small, ,, 3", ,, 5", | 1/6 |

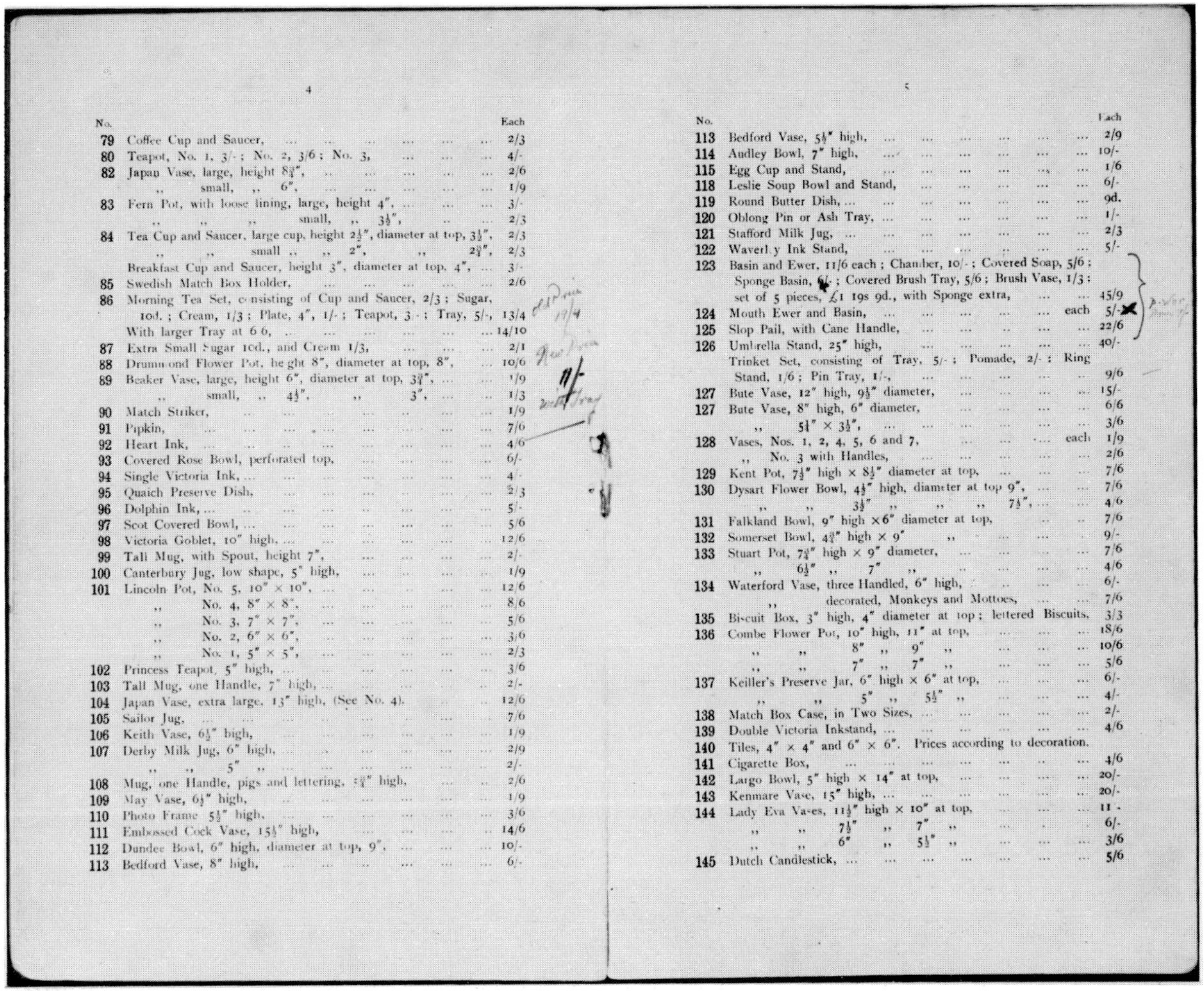

4

| No. | | Each |
|---|---|---|
| 79 | Coffee Cup and Saucer, ... ... ... ... ... ... | 2/3 |
| 80 | Teapot, No. 1, 3/- ; No. 2, 3/6 ; No. 3, ... ... ... | 4/- |
| 82 | Japan Vase, large, height 8¾", .. ... ... ... ... | 2/6 |
| | ,, small, ,, 6", ... ... ... ... ... | 1/9 |
| 83 | Fern Pot, with loose lining, large, height 4", ... ... ... | 3/- |
| | ,, ,, ,, small, ,, 3½", .. ... | 2/3 |
| 84 | Tea Cup and Saucer, large cup, height 2½", diameter at top, 3½", | 2/3 |
| | ,, ,, small ,, ,, 2", ,, 2¾", | 2/3 |
| | Breakfast Cup and Saucer, height 3", diameter at top, 4", ... | 3/- |
| 85 | Swedish Match Box Holder, ... ... ... ... ... | 2/6 |
| 86 | Morning Tea Set, consisting of Cup and Saucer, 2/3 ; Sugar, 10d. ; Cream, 1/3 ; Plate, 4", 1/- ; Teapot, 3/- ; Tray, 5/-, | 13/4 |
| | With larger Tray at 6/6, .. ... ... ... ... ... | 14/10 |
| 87 | Extra Small Sugar 10d., and Cream 1/3, ... ... ... | 2/1 |
| 88 | Drummond Flower Pot, height 8", diameter at top, 8", ... | 10/6 |
| 89 | Beaker Vase, large, height 6", diameter at top, 3¾", ... ... | 1/9 |
| | ,, small, ,, 4½", ,, 3", ... ... | 1/3 |
| 90 | Match Striker, .. ... ... ... .. ... ... | 1/9 |
| 91 | Pipkin, ... ... ... ... ... ... ... ... | 7/6 |
| 92 | Heart Ink, ... .. .. ... ... ... ... ... | 4/6 |
| 93 | Covered Rose Bowl, perforated top, ... ... ... ... | 6/- |
| 94 | Single Victoria Ink, ... ... ... ... ... ... ... | 4/- |
| 95 | Quaich Preserve Dish, ... ... ... ... ... ... | 2/3 |
| 96 | Dolphin Ink, ... .. ... ... ... ... ... ... | 5/- |
| 97 | Scot Covered Bowl, ... ... ... ... ... ... ... | 5/6 |
| 98 | Victoria Goblet, 10" high, ... ... ... ... ... ... | 12/6 |
| 99 | Tall Mug, with Spout, height 7", ... ... ... ... | 2/- |
| 100 | Canterbury Jug, low shape, 5" high, ... ... ... ... | 1/9 |
| 101 | Lincoln Pot, No. 5, 10" × 10", ... ... ... ... ... | 12/6 |
| | ,, No. 4, 8" × 8", ... ... ... ... ... | 8/6 |
| | ,, No. 3, 7" × 7", ... ... ... ... ... | 5/6 |
| | ,, No. 2, 6" × 6", ... ... ... ... ... | 3/6 |
| | ,, No. 1, 5" × 5", ... ... ... ... ... | 2/3 |
| 102 | Princess Teapot, 5" high, ... ... ... ... ... ... | 3/6 |
| 103 | Tall Mug, one Handle, 7" high, ... ... ... .. | 2/- |
| 104 | Japan Vase, extra large, 13" high, (See No. 4). ... .. | 12/6 |
| 105 | Sailor Jug, ... ... ... ... ... ... ... ... | 7/6 |
| 106 | Keith Vase, 6½" high, ... ... ... ... ... ... | 1/9 |
| 107 | Derby Milk Jug, 6" high, ... .. ... ... ... ... | 2/9 |
| | ,, ,, 5" ,, ... ... ... ... ... | 2/- |
| 108 | Mug, one Handle, pigs and lettering, 2¾" high, ... ... | 2/6 |
| 109 | May Vase, 6½" high, ... ... ... ... ... ... | 1/9 |
| 110 | Photo Frame 5½" high, ... ... ... ... ... ... | 3/6 |
| 111 | Embossed Cock Vase, 15½" high, ... ... ... .. | 14/6 |
| 112 | Dundee Bowl, 6" high, diameter at top, 9", ... ... ... | 10/- |
| 113 | Bedford Vase, 8" high, ... ... .. ... ... ... | 6/- |

5

| No. | | Each |
|---|---|---|
| 113 | Bedford Vase, 5½" high, ... ... ... ... ... ... | 2/9 |
| 114 | Audley Bowl, 7" high, ... ... ... ... ... ... | 10/- |
| 115 | Egg Cup and Stand, ... ... ... ... ... ... | 1/6 |
| 118 | Leslie Soup Bowl and Stand, ... ... ... ... ... | 6/- |
| 119 | Round Butter Dish, ... ... ... ... ... ... ... | 9d. |
| 120 | Oblong Pin or Ash Tray, ... ... ... ... ... ... | 1/- |
| 121 | Stafford Milk Jug, ... ... ... ... ... ... ... | 2/3 |
| 122 | Waverley Ink Stand, ... ... ... .. ... ... | 5/- |
| 123 | Basin and Ewer, 11/6 each ; Chamber, 10/- ; Covered Soap, 5/6 ; Sponge Basin, 6/- ; Covered Brush Tray, 5/6 ; Brush Vase, 1/3 ; set of 5 pieces, £1 19s 9d., with Sponge extra, ... ... | 45/9 |
| 124 | Mouth Ewer and Basin, ... ... ... ... ... each | 5/- |
| 125 | Slop Pail, with Cane Handle, ... ... .. ... ... | 22/6 |
| 126 | Umbrella Stand, 25" high, ... ... ... ... ... | 40/- |
| | Trinket Set, consisting of Tray, 5/- ; Pomade, 2/- ; Ring Stand, 1/6 ; Pin Tray, 1/-, ... ... ... ... .. | 9/6 |
| 127 | Bute Vase, 12" high, 9½" diameter, ... ... ... ... | 15/- |
| 127 | Bute Vase, 8" high, 6" diameter, ... ... ... ... | 6/6 |
| | ,, 5¼" × 3½", ... ... ... ... ... ... ... | 3/6 |
| 128 | Vases, Nos. 1, 2, 4, 5, 6 and 7, ... ... ... each | 1/9 |
| | ,, No. 3 with Handles, ... ... ... ... ... | 2/6 |
| 129 | Kent Pot, 7½" high × 8½" diameter at top, ... ... ... | 7/6 |
| 130 | Dysart Flower Bowl, 4½" high, diameter at top 9", ... ... | 7/6 |
| | ,, ,, 3½" ,, ,, ,, 7½", ... ... | 4/6 |
| 131 | Falkland Bowl, 9" high × 6" diameter at top, .. .. | 7/6 |
| 132 | Somerset Bowl, 4¾" high × 9" ,, ... ... | 9/- |
| 133 | Stuart Pot, 7¾" high × 9" diameter, ... ... ... | 7/6 |
| | ,, 6½" ,, 7" ,, .. ... ... ... | 4/6 |
| 134 | Waterford Vase, three Handled, 6" high, .. ... ... | 6/- |
| | ,, decorated, Monkeys and Mottoes, ... ... | 7/6 |
| 135 | Biscuit Box, 3" high, 4" diameter at top ; lettered Biscuits, | 3/3 |
| 136 | Combe Flower Pot, 10" high, 11" at top, ... ... .. | 18/6 |
| | ,, ,, 8" ,, 9" ,, ... ... ... | 10/6 |
| | ,, ,, 7" ,, 7" ,, ... ... ... | 5/6 |
| 137 | Keiller's Preserve Jar, 6" high × 6" at top, ... ... ... | 6/- |
| | ,, ,, 5" ,, 5½" ,, ... ... ... | 4/- |
| 138 | Match Box Case, in Two Sizes, ... ... ... ... ... | 2/- |
| 139 | Double Victoria Inkstand, ... ... ... ... ... ... | 4/6 |
| 140 | Tiles, 4" × 4" and 6" × 6". Prices according to decoration. | |
| 141 | Cigarette Box, ... ... ... ... ... .. ... | 4/6 |
| 142 | Largo Bowl, 5" high × 14" at top, ... ... ... ... | 20/- |
| 143 | Kenmare Vase, 15" high, ... ... ... ... ... ... | 20/- |
| 144 | Lady Eva Vases, 11½" high × 10" at top, ... ... ... | 11/- |
| | ,, ,, 7½" ,, 7" ,, ... . . | 6/- |
| | ,, ,, 6" ,, 5½" ,, ... ... ... | 3/6 |
| 145 | Dutch Candlestick, ... ... ... ... ... ... ... | 5/6 |

The Fife Flower Bowl becomes a dog or a puss bowl with the addition of the appropriate lettering (list Nos. 12 and 18) (Plates 63 and 170).

Many of the pots were made in a selection of sizes; they are generally listed under one entry number but with the various sizes often shown in inches.

Bedroom ware could be painted to match wall papers and any pot painted with a black ground was quoted at fifteen per cent extra.

Several items found by collectors do not appear in any price list we have seen. These are generally pieces which were made for special events:

Commemorative ware:
  60th Jubilee of Queen Victoria (1897).
  Boer War (1901).
  Coronation of King Edward VII and
    Queen Alexandra (June 1902,
    postponed due to the King's illness).
  Coronation of King Edward VII and
    Queen Alexandra (August 1902).
  Coronation of King George V and
    Queen Mary (1911).

Other items:
  'Beadle of Perth' Jug.
  'Fair Maid of Perth' Jug.
  Tea Kettle.

| No. | | Each |
|---|---|---|
| 146 | Squat Beaker, | 3/- |
| 147 | Dorset Jug, ... | 2 6 |
| 148 | Dalkeith Bowl, | 6/- |
| 149 | Edinburgh Candlestick, | 5/6 |
| 150 | Three Handled Beaker, | 5/- |
| 151 | Kinghorn Vase, ... | 7/6 |
| 152 | Argyle Vase, ... | 7/- |
| 153 | Table Napkin Ring, | 1/6 |
| 154 | Fish, ... | 40/- |
| 155 | Dunblane Candlestick, | 4/- |
| 156 | Stoup, ... | 2/6 |
| 157 | Norfolk Vase, | 11/6 |
| 158 | Stanley Jug, | 2/6 |
| 159 | Daisy Candlestick, | 2/6 |
| 160 | Doune Candlestick, | 4/- |
| 161 | Lady Eva Tray, | 1/6 |
| 162 | Cheese Stand, Two Sizes, ... 6/- and | 4/6 |
| 163 | Douglas Vase, | 1/9 |
| 164 | Ian Candlestick, | 3/- |
| 165 | Lady Sybil Vase, ... | 3/- |
| 166 | Lemon Squeezer, | 2/6 |
| 167 | Oban Candlestick, ... | 4/- |
| 168 | Spill Vase, | 9d. |
| 169 | Keswick Vase, ... | 1/9 |
| 170 | Salve Box, ... | 1/3 |

NOT IN ILLUSTRATED SHEET.

| No. | | Each |
|---|---|---|
| 171 | Pres. Jar, Fruit Knob, | 4/- |
| 172 | New Honey Jar, | 7/6 |
| 173 | Square Fruit Dishes,—L.S., 6.6 ; M.S., 4/6 ; S.S., ... | 1/9 |
| 174 | Delvaux Bowl, | 3 6 |
| | ,, Outside Decoration only, ... | 1/9 |
| | ,, ,, with Cover, ... | 2/6 |
| 175 | Individual Pres. Jar, | 2/- |
| 176 | 3" Plate as Stand, | 9d. |
| 177 | Dessert Ware, Usual Decoration— | |
| | Gordon Dessert Plate, ... | 2/6 |
| | Low Comport, ... | 6/6 |
| | Tall Comport, ... | 8/6 |

7

| No. | | Each |
|---|---|---|
| | 18 piece Set consisting of— | |
| | 12 Plates, 4 Low and 2 Tall Comports, ... | £3 13/- |
| 12 | Fife Flower Bowl, same as Dog Bowl but without Mottoes, | |
| | 5/-, 3/3 and | 1/9 |
| 178 | Oval Pin Box, | 2/- |

SPECIAL DECORATIONS TO ORDER.

Bedroom Ware, etc., quoted for, to match Wall Papers ; and also in Apple Green and Pink Glazes, with Monogram or Crest in White Enamel.

Decorations on Black Ground, about 15% dearer than above List.

WEMYSS DECORATIONS ON CHINA.

| | | |
|---|---|---|
| TEA WARE.—Sets of 21 pieces (6" Muffins), | ... | £2 1 10 |
| ,, 40 pieces ,, | ... | 3 17 2 |
| Teas and Saucers, 3/2 each, C. & S. | | |
| Muffins, 6", - 2/2 ,, | | |
| Cream, - 3/1 ,, | | |
| Sugar, - 3/2 ,, | | |
| B. & B. Plate, - 3/4 ,, | | |

This early photograph, showing shapes Nos. 98 to 126, is the surviving remnant of the first printed Wemyss catalogue.

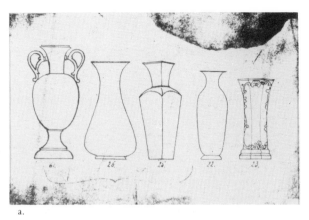

a.

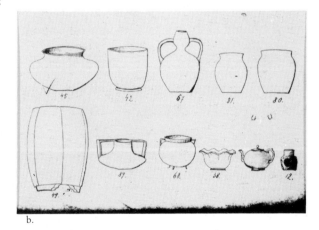

b.

a. & b. Sketches for an early catalogue. All of the shapes illustrated here have been seen by the authors. Some of the shapes were not developed and do not appear in later catalogues.

a.

b.

a. & b. Two photographs illustrating shapes, which have survived with the catalogue issued to herald the 1920s.

Throughout the text, and in the captions to the photographs, we have generally been able to use the name given by the Fife Pottery for each pot. There are, however, a number of vases, candlesticks and bowls to which we have not been able to assign names. Some of these pieces were probably unpopular and rarely asked for.

Several of the candlesticks listed in the Fife Pottery Catalogue cannot be identified, as some of the photographic sheets are missing.

This photograph illustrates some of the candlesticks known to the authors. Only one of these we cannot name.

CANDLESTICKS
Top row. Left to right.
a. Extra Tall
b. Antique
c. Tall Kintore
d. 7″ Square Base
e. Nairn

Bottom row. Left to right.
f. Low Kintore
g. Duchess
h. Dalmeny
i. Unidentified

# XII. CHRONOLOGY

David Methven & Sons, Kirkcaldy Pottery.
Robert Heron & Son, Fife Pottery, Kirkcaldy.

1714  William Adam and his father-in-law, William Robertson, begin manufacturing bricks and tiles in the Linkton of Abbotshall, Kirkcaldy.

1739  Elizabeth Stocks born at Kinghorn.

c.1740  David Methven born, probably in north-east Fife.

c.1770  David Methven marries Elizabeth Stocks.

1772  John Methven born at Kinghorn.

1775  David Methven (2nd) born at Abbotshall (d. 1815).

1776  David Methven purchases Brick and Tile works at Linkton of Abbotshall from John Adam, Architect. Brown Ware Pottery being made.

1783  George Methven born.

1790  Gallatown Pottery operating. Owned by 'Gray & Co.', Potters. c. 1812.

1798  David Methven (3rd), son of David (2nd) born.

1799  Robert Heron born.

1802  John Methven, Potter, marries Mary Moodie at Parish of Cannongate.

1804  Their son David (4th) born at Abbotshall.

1805  Their daughter Mary born at Abbotshall.

c.1809  John Methven is already producing pottery in a building adjacent to his father's brick and tile works.

1817  Gray & Co., Potters, build a large new pottery which they rename 'The Fife Pottery'.

1822  Andrew and Archibald Gray, of Gray & Co., Potters, take out a bond, with the Fife Pottery as Security.

1826  Gray & Co., Potters at Fife Pottery, and [the late] Andrew, and Archibald Gray, the partners, have their estate sequestrated and the bankrupt pottery is advertised for sale.

1827  David Methven (1st) dies of old age and debility 'aged 80 to 100' and was buried at Abbotshall in a 'sief' (safe). He leaves the ground, on which his son John had built a pottery, to John, and the Brick and Tile works to his remaining son George with a sum of money to his grandson David (3rd).

John Methven purchases the Fife Pottery.

1828  Mary Methven marries Robert Heron.

1833  Robert Methven Heron born at Dysart.

1837  David Methven (4th), son of John, dies. John Methven dies, leaving the Links Pottery and the Fife Pottery to his daughter Mary Methven Heron and his son-in-law Robert Heron.

c.1837  Robert and Mary Heron sell the Links Pottery to George Methven.

1847  George Methven dies, leaving the Links Pottery and Brick and Tile works to his nephew David Methven (3rd).

1857  David Methven (3rd) testifies in the Court of Session that he has produced Brown Ware for the past forty years and that his ancestors had been producing it for the past eighty years at least.

1862  David Methven (5th), son of David (3rd), dies.

1864  David Methven (3rd) dies leaving Links Pottery and Brick and Tile works to his son James and the family of his late son David.

James Methven purchases the Links Pottery and Brick and Tile works from his brother's widow and family.

1869  Robert Heron dies.

c.1883  Karel Nekola is employed as a decorator at Fife Pottery.

1887  Mary Methven dies, leaving Fife Pottery to her son Robert Methven Heron and his sister Jessie.

James Methven takes his pottery manager, Andrew Young, into partnership. By now the name of the Links Pottery has been changed to the Kirkcaldy Pottery.

1892  James Methven dies and the Kirkcaldy Pottery and the Brick and Tile works are sold to Andrew Young and his sons.

1895  Jessie Heron dies.

1906  Robert Methven Heron dies and leaves the Fife Pottery to his friend, William Williamson, Merchant.

1915  Karel Nekola dies at Dysart.

Andrew Young dies at Abbotshall, leaving the Kirkcaldy Pottery to his sons.

1916    Edwin Sandland appointed chief decorator at Fife Pottery.

1928    Edwin Sandland dies.
Joseph Nekola appointed chief decorator at Fife Pottery.

1930    The Fife Pottery and the Kirkcaldy Pottery close.

Acknowledgements to: Scottish Record Office, Edinburgh; Register House, Edinburgh; The National Library of Scotland, Edinburgh; Kirkcaldy Public Library; Clackmannan County Library; British Museum Reading Room, London.

Historical research by Robert Rankine.

## XIII. REFERENCES

Only easily accessible references are cited here. Obscurer ones can be found in the text of our book and are cited in the Index.

J. Arnold Fleming, *Scottish Pottery*, 299 pp. (1923: reprinted 1973).

The Scottish Arts Council, *Wemyss Ware: the development of a decorative Scottish Pottery, c.1883–1930*, 20 pp. (Catalogue to Exhibition, Edinburgh, 1971).

Frank Hamer, *The Potter's Dictionary of Materials and Techniques* (Pitman & Black, 1975).

Rogers de Rin, *Wemyss Ware, c.1880–1930*, 136 pp. (Illustrated Catalogue, 1976).

'A Natural Delight.' Exhibition at Huntly House Museum, Edinburgh (1981).

# WEMYSS WARE.

## THE
# ORIGINAL HAND-PAINTED POTTERY
— IN —
## FLOWERS, FRUITS, COCKS AND HENS,
### AND OTHER DECORATIONS.

SOLE MAKERS—
# ROBERT HERON & SON,
## KIRKCALDY.

# R.H.&S.Fife Pottery

Wemyss Ware evolved over a period of years and as a result of various influences. Robert Heron, whose family owned the Fife Pottery was himself an artist and surely the driving force behind the development of the style. Although 1882 appears to be the year when Wemyss Ware was first sold under that name, both the Fife Pottery and the Links Pottery in Kirkcaldy produced decorated ware for many years before then. Some of the products of Heron's Pottery closely resembled Wemyss Ware, as Robert Heron experimented, not only with the techniques but also with the style.

**2.** Loving cup: Red nasturtiums — a step nearer to Wemyss Ware but the borders are experimental.

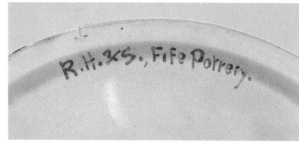

**1.** Loving cup: Garlands of small yellow roses and forget-me-nots under a swagged and fringed curtain, reflecting the Victorian taste for velvet and tassels. This is an experimental piece showing the Wemyss style emerging. The roses are brush-painted but the petals on the drapes have been applied by sponge.

**3.** Both loving cups are inscribed in red 'R. H. & S., Fife Pottery'. The word Wemyss is not yet in use as a name for the ware and in our opinion these pieces were decorated *c.* 1880.

53

## Sources and competitors

The Links Pottery, renamed the Kirkcaldy Pottery *c.* 1887, was owned by the Methven family, although by then in partnership with Andrew Young. They produced various lines in competition with the Fife Pottery, including Abbotsford Ware, Nisbet Ware, Auld Heather Ware and Airlie Ware. Gilding occurs very rarely on impressed Wemyss – the Comb Tray with a basket of flowers being one such rarity. However, the gilded cheese dishes, jugs and teapots are good examples of this technique which predates Wemyss and may serve to demonstrate how Robert Heron was striving to establish a style. Many of the pre-Wemyss decorations were continued in a more sophisticated way on the new ware, but without the gilding.

\* Denotes unmarked piece

**5.** Comb tray: Basket of stylised forget-me-nots with gilded border.

54

**4.** Cheese stands: a. Grey wagtail.\*
b. Heron.\* c. Stork.\* d. Jug: Goldfinches.\* e. Teapot: Grapes.\*
f. Teapot: Robin.\* All the pots on this plate are from the general range and are lightly gilded. These shapes are also to be found in the Wemyss range.

**7.** A selection of marked Abbotsford ware from David Methven & Sons. a. Preserve jar: Roses. b. Bowl: Roses. c. Plate: Pears. d. Mug with two handles: Brown cock and hen.
e. Preserve jar: Black cock and hen.

**6.** a. Large preserve jar: Stag with deer.\*
b. Mug: Fox hunt with fox and hounds.\*
These are unmarked items, possibly from the pottery of David Methven.

## Local Landmarks

Once a busy port, Dysart carried on so much trade with the Netherlands that the town was known as 'Little Holland'. Near the harbour is the ruined church of St Serf with its tall tower dating from the early sixteenth century. On the cliffs east of Dysart and West Wemyss stands the Castle of Wemyss, parts of which date from the thirteenth century. The castle commands superb views of the Firth of Forth looking over to Edinburgh and the Braid Hills.

The young Karel Nekola soon explored the surroundings of his new home in Kirkcaldy and chose these two historic buildings as the focal points for these beautifully painted plaques. One of them carries Nekola's initials and the date 1883.

**8.** Plaque: Dysart with St Serf's Church Tower. Signed 'KN' and dated 1883.

**9.** Plaque: Wemyss Castle, West Wemyss.

# 'Who is the Potter, pray, and who the Pot?'

EDWARD FITZGERALD

## EVOLVING SHAPES

Most of the early Wemyss shapes were striving for originality and identity. The more obvious influences include Chinese, Roman, Greek and Staffordshire.

It should be remembered, of course, that Peter Gardner, working at the Dunmore Pottery near Airth, already enjoyed a considerable reputation under the patronage of the Countess of Dunmore for his superb glazes and potting techniques. Early self-coloured Wemyss sometimes bears a striking resemblance to Dunmore ware. This would be no accident, but a deliberate effort to obtain a share of the profitable market.

**10.** a. Rustic teapot: mazarine blue with white enamelled flowers.* b. Plate: green glaze with quotation from Burns in white enamel. c. Vase: green glaze with white enamelled flowers.

**11.** a. Vase: yellow glaze. b. Vase: yellow glaze. c. Cheese dish: red glaze with white enamelled flowers.*
d. Rustic jet teapot with inscription in white enamel.*

**13.** a. Palm pot (21″ diam.): yellow glaze b. Vase: yellow glaze. c. 'Baluster' vase: green glaze. d. Vase with two handles: crimson glaze.

**14.** a. Bowl: crimson glaze.
b. Nairn candlestick: crimson glaze.
c. Plaque with design of impressed leaves.
d. Vase: green glaze.
e. Bowl: yellow glaze with incised design including fox, geese and chickens, with background of leaves.

**12.** Large 'Gypsy' pot mottled dark blue and red.

## The Chinese Connection

A few major pieces exist in the Chinese style, either in terms of decoration or of shape. Unfortunately, the concept was not sustained, probably because it was too costly and too time-consuming to develop profitably. Some of the larger items were listed in the catalogues until the Fife Pottery closed, but the Baluster vase does not appear in any printed list we have seen.

**16.** A pair of panelled vases: Chinoiserie design with Mandarins, dragons, chrysanthemums and bamboos. H22″.

**15.** Baluster vase: Chinoiserie design on yellow ground, H21″.

**17.** Fish: modelled from a Chinese porcelain carp at Wemyss Castle, length 19″.

**18.** Chinese garden seat: exotic birds, red lilies and palms. This piece has an oval impressed mark which reads:

Wemyss Ware
R. Heron
Fife Pottery

**19.** Chinese garden seat: foxgloves, chrysanthemums and campion. Mark as Plate **18.**

The Garden seats are 18″ high.

**20.** Chinese garden seat: chrysanthemums and Vitex agnus-casti with exotic butterflies and grasses. This item has a painted mark but the name 'Wemyss' is not present, thus suggesting a date earlier than 1882. The mark reads:

Robert Heron & Son
Kirkcaldy
Fife Pottery    NB

# 'He best can paint them who shall feel them most'
ALEXANDER POPE

## A STYLE OF PAINTING

What were Robert Heron and his team of decorators trying to achieve? Commercial considerations apart, the objectives appear to have been originality, a fresh approach to decorating pottery, and the creation of pieces to give pleasure and add colour and interest to their surroundings.

Much Wemyss Ware was produced for decorative rather than purely functional purposes, but most pieces were expected to satisfy both criteria. Karel Nekola often sketched his subjects before painting the pots, and we illustrate here two good examples of his work, presumably drawn from nature.

**21.** a. Narcissus. Pen and ink sketch on paper.
b. Daffodils. Pen and ink sketch on paper, watercoloured.

**22.** Pen and ink sketch on paper: Iris. Plates **21** and **22** are original sketches by Karel Nekola, used in the Fife Pottery as a guide in decorating. Some are found, like the daffodil sketch here, with the outlines pinholed for stencilling.

**23.** a. Stuart pot: roses in a diamond pattern on a black ground. b. Vase: green glaze. c. Combe flower-pot: chrysanthemums on a black ground. d. Tile: green cockerel.

**24.** a. Jet teapot* from general range with inscription and enamelled flowers. b. Rothes flower-pot: daffodils on a black background. c. Vase: lilac on black ground. d. Bowl: geese on a black ground.

## 'My heart's in the Highlands a-chasing the deer ...'
ROBERT BURNS

## A ROYAL STAG ROARING
A magnificent stag challenges his rival. The painting, almost certainly by Karel Nekola, is carefully executed and a splendid example of the artist's ability to paint natural subjects with movement and depth.

A royal stag should, of course, have at least twelve points to his antlers. These beasts just fail to qualify, but have impeccable royal connections. They live at Balmoral and may have delighted Queen Victoria herself.

**26a.** Balmoral Castle.

**25, 26.** Tub flower-pot: stags by a highland burn.

Reproduced by gracious permission of Her Majesty the Queen.

*'O lovely Pussy! O Pussy, my love*
*What a beautiful Pussy you are!'*

EDWARD LEAR

Wemyss cats are delightful and not easy to find
in the open market, especially with original
glass eyes and impressed mark on base.
If decorated with hearts and roundels on a
yellow ground, they bear a passing
resemblance to Gallé cats, but Heron's cats are
hard to beat – and they appear to know it!

**28.** Yellow glaze decorated in the
manner of a Gallé cat.

**30.** Tabby cat.

## CATS

**27.** a. Yellow
glaze.
b. Tabby cat.

**29.** a. Green glaze.
b. Puss bowl: apples.

# 'A cat may look on a king'

JOHN HAYWOOD

**31.** a. Keith vase: shamrock.
b. Gordon dessert plate: shamrock.
c. Pig: shamrock. d. Cat: shamrock.

**32.** Two cats* with gilt fur sporting pink ribbons. These are from the general range.

**33.** a. Cat* with pink ribbons.
b. Cat: pink glaze.
c. Carafe: pink ribbons with crown and monogram Edward VII and Queen Alexandra.
d. Heart tray: pink ribbons with crown and monogram: Queen Victoria's Diamond Jubilee, 1897.
e. Tall Quaich (small): pink ribbons.

## The Cat, the Kitten and the Canary

Painted cats and kittens are very rare, but the canary plaque may be the only one of its kind – a copy of seventeenth-century Dutch Delft plaque and a charming example of the artist's ability to achieve a three-dimensional effect on a flat pottery surface.

**35.** Plaque: canary in a cage. Initialled 'KN', 12·5″ wide.

**36.** Match striker: Kittens in grass.

**34.** Horn tumbler: black cat.

**37.** Detail of the match striker.

*'Human speech is like a cracked kettle on which we tap crude rhythms*
*for bears to dance to, while we long to make music that will melt the stars'*
GUSTAVE FLAUBERT (MADAME BOVARY)

## MONKEYS AND BEARS

The dancing bears illustrated here are the only
Wemyss bears known to the authors. They are
a splendid example of original decorating,
evocative of Bohemia: this could well be a
piece painted by Karel Nekola for his children.
The Three Wise Monkeys tend to look like
hairy old men. Although rare, examples are
still to be found with various members of the
trio both under and in the tree.

**39.** Pin tray.

The three wise monkeys. Hear no evil, see no
evil, speak no evil. The legend relates to the
'Three Wise Monkeys' carved over the door
of the Sacred Stable, Nikko, Japan.

**38.** Comb tray: dancing bears with a melodeon.

**40.** Loving cup.

**41.** Single Princess Inkstand.

*'If it had grown up,' she said to herself,*
*'it would have made a dreadfully ugly child;*
*but it makes rather a handsome pig, I think'*
LEWIS CARROLL – ALICE'S ADVENTURES IN WONDERLAND

## PIGS

Wemyss pigs were made with the nursery or
the bedroom in mind. The big ones were
sometimes used as doorstops, which no
doubt accounts for the high incidence of
broken tails and chipped ears.
The little ones were occasionally made with
a slot in their backs for use as piggy banks.
Sometimes a child's name and birth-date
were inscribed alongside – a personalised pig.
Some highly prized piglets lie asleep on their
sides and were used as paper-weights. Others
have a hole in their snouts for whisky to be
poured into, prior to use as 'first footing'
bottles.
Large pigs are usually very handsome, and
the earliest ones have particularly deeply
etched lines around the face and chin, giving
them a delightfully worried look.

**43.** Large pig: roses, thistles and shamrock.

**45.** Two small pigs in green and pink glazes
with a large pig decorated with roses.

**42.** Large pig: black on white with a
family of small pigs.

**44.** Small pigs: roses. These are money banks
and have been specially decorated for
two lucky children.

**46.** Small pig:
dark blue
glaze.

66

# 'To market, to market, to buy a fat pig'

ANON

**47.** Three small pigs with a large white glazed pig. In addition to an impressed mark, this pig has Fife Pottery incised into its base and is obviously early. Note the well-defined features.

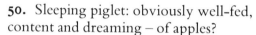

**49.** Large pig: shamrock with two small pigs, shamrock and green glaze.

**51.** Two small pigs: mauve glaze.

**50.** Sleeping piglet: obviously well-fed, content and dreaming – of apples?

**48.** Two small black and white pigs, one with an open snout to be used as a bottle, and a sleeping piglet: thistles.

# FARM ANIMALS

Although the countryside was the inspiration for much of the decoration, farm animals are uncommon and invariably painted in lush Summer pastures.

**52.** Grosvenor vase: cows in field.

**54.** Mug: cows in field.

**55.** Mug: pigs in field.

**56.** a. Mug: pigs with inscription 'They grew in beauty side by side'. b. Square tray: pig in field. c. Heart tray: sheep in field. d. Grosvenor vase: cows in meadow.

**57.** Butter tub: bull in field with cows on reverse.

**53.** Matchbox case: sheep with lamb.

# ANIMAL SCENES

Nekola's drawings of rabbits illustrate his concern for movement and accuracy. Although Wemyss animal scenes are rare, he invariably succeeds in capturing the essential character of the creatures.

**59**

**60**

**61**

**58**

**62**

**58.** Embossed cock vase: chamois on mountainside.

**59.** Mug: stag.

**60.** Chesham fern pot: hares in meadow.

**61.** Comb tray: ponies on hillside.

**62.** Watercolour sketches of rabbits, pinholed for stencilling.

# RARE WEMYSS ANIMALS

Only one pair of bulldogs is known to the Authors. Both dogs are unmarked, but unmistakably bred from a long line of Wemyss roses.

**64.** Rabbit: white glaze with black patches. The red-eyed rabbit is the only one known to the authors.

**63.** a. Bulldog:* roses. The bulldog is open underneath and is very light. These have been bought in as biscuit ware for decoration in the Fife Pottery.

**(63)** b. Dog bowl: roses with inscription.

*'How doth the little busy bee*
*Improve each shining hour,*
*And gather honey all the day*
*From every opening flower!'*

ISAAC WATTS

## BEES AND HONEY POTS

Bees buzzed around Wemyss honey pots and skeps for at least fifty years, *c.* 1885–1930. One particularly popular version was the square honeycomb box with thistle knopped lid, supplied complete with drip tray which was made to Thomas Goode's specification. Thomas Goode, an internationally renowned retailer in Mayfair, supplied pottery and porcelain to the well-to-do.

**66.** a. Plate: honeysuckle with visiting bees. b. Preserve jar: beehive with bees. Note the (early) red swagged rim to pot and cover.

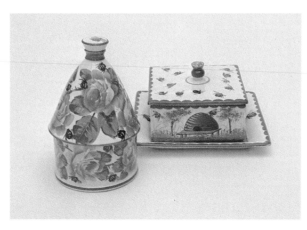

**65.** a. Honey jar in the shape of a bee skep: roses. This shape may be a late, but nonetheless attractive design b. Covered honey box with drip tray: beehive and bees in orchard.

**67.** a. Low quaich dessert dish. b. Honey jar in shape of bee skep. c. Covered honey box with tray. d. Preserve jar. e. Individual preserve jar. This small pot was made specifically for the breakfast tray.

**68.** Honey jar in form of bee skep.

71

## DRAGONFLIES AND BUTTERFLIES

Various insects occur in Wemyss decoration. Caterpillars, ladybirds, grasshoppers and butterflies are rare: dragonflies and bees are more easily discovered and keenly collected.

**69.** Wash-set complete with slop-pail and Duchess Candlesticks. Dragonflies over reeded pond. (Painted by James Sharp.)

**70.** Detail of decoration on slop-pail.

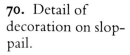

**72.** Ewer and basin: butterflies over pond, painted by Edwin Sandland.

**71.** Japan vase: dragonflies over water.

# DRAGONFLIES IN PROFUSION

**73.** a. Plates. b. Cups and saucers. c. Comb tray. d. Covered jug. e. Sugar. (All painted by James Sharp.)

**74.** a. Chesham fern pot. b. Lincoln pot. c. Vase. d. Low pomade. e. May vase. f. Beaker vase. g. Spill vase.

**75.** Heart tray: aerial acrobatics, painted by Karel Nekola.

## 'The Cock, that is the trumpet to the morn'

WILLIAM SHAKESPEARE – HAMLET

Cock and hen painting appears to have been very popular. Among other potteries, Pountney & Co., of Bristol also produced a range of black cock-and-hen ware, usually painted by George Stewart.

None can compare, however, with the best examples of Wemyss fowl, which are normally black (Leghorns?) or brown (Rhode Island Reds?) and, rarely, grey.

**77.** Comb tray: black cock and two hens with the inscription 'There's news, lassies, news!'.

**78.** Stationery rack:* black cock and hen.

**79.** a. Gypsy flower-pot: black cock and hen. b. Porridge saucer: black cock. Note the unusual moulded border of leaves.

**80.** Heart inkstand: black cock and hen.

**76.** Comb tray: black and brown cockerel with a grey hen. The tray is initialled 'KN' and is a fine example of Nekola's free-hand painting.

74

*'. . . how much louder a cock can crow
in its own farmyard'*

**81, 82.** Mug: two black cockerels.

**81**

**82**

**83.** a. Mug: black cock-and-hen design. Note the grass applied by sponge together with the red detailing which suggest that this is an early piece. b. Elgin vase: black cocks and hens with some roosting on a branch. c. Comb tray: black cockerel with inscription. d. Low pomade: black cockerel. e. Porridge saucer: black cockerel. f. Tall quaich (small): black cockerel.

**84.** Loving cup: a vigorous design of black cocks and hens. Note the red detailing and compare it with Plate **2**.

75

## 'A cock has great influence on his own dunghill'

PUBLICIUS SYRUS – MAXIMS

**85.** a. Heart tray: brown cocks and hens. b. Mug: brown cocks and hens.

**86.** Embossed cock vase: brown cockerel catching a fly.

**86**

**87.** a. Loving cup: brown cocks and hens. b. Egg cup: brown hens. c. Invalid feeding cup: brown cocks and hens.

d. Mug: brown cock and hen design. e. Gypsy flower-pot: brown cock and hen design.

76

**88.** Loving cup: brown cock and hen design. A further example from the early days of Wemyss Ware.

*'Christmas is coming, the geese are getting fat,*
*please put a penny in the old man's hat.*
*If you haven't got a penny a ha'penny will do,*
*If you haven't got a ha'penny, God bless you.'*

The sketch of geese once again demonstrates concern for movement and character in the painting of living creatures. The turkey is very rare and makes an exciting, if somewhat bizarre decoration on a Grosvenor vase.

**89.** Grosvenor vase: turkey (in Scotland, a 'Bubbly-Jock').

**90.** Loving cup: geese feeding.

**91.** Two tiles
a. Geese
b. Black hen with chicks.

**93.** Pencil sketch of geese. This sketch, almost certainly the work of Karel Nekola, is not signed, as it was intended for use in the decorating shop.

 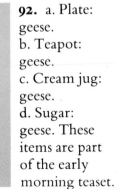

**92.** a. Plate: geese.
b. Teapot: geese.
c. Cream jug: geese.
d. Sugar: geese. These items are part of the early morning teaset.

# ORNAMENTAL AND OTHER BIRDS

Elegant country house peacocks, exotic tropical birds, a sandmartin and a heron about to do severe damage to himself or to some unsuspecting fish . . . just some of the many delightful inhabitants of the Wemyss aviary.

**94.** Mug: peacock with tail trailing.

**95.** Japan vase: peacock sitting in branch.

**97.** a. Japan vase: heron fishing. b. Beaker vase: sandmartin with dragonflies over pool. c. Bowl: pool with carp and yellow water-lilies.

**96.** Mug: peacock with tail in display.

**98.** Chamber-pot: exotic blue flowers with exotic birds.

# MALLARD IN THE WILD

Mallard drakes – and very occasionally ducks –
are highly prized by Wemyss collectors.
Mallard wash-sets may be particularly action-
packed with birds taking off in alarm from
clumps of reeds.

99

100

**99.** Mug: ducks swimming on pond.

**100.** Mug: mallard feeding.

**101.** Ewer and basin: mallard in
flight over pond, painted by Karel
Nekola.

**102.** a. Tall pomade: mallard over
reed-bed. b. Grosvenor vase: mallard
landing, painted by Karel Nekola.

101

102

103

**103.** Tub flower pot: Mallard in flight
over pond.

**104.** Loving cup: Mallard over pond.

104

# GAME BIRDS

The monogram HP appears on a number of interesting pieces. The authors believe this may have been Harry Primrose, Lord Dalmeny, Fifth Earl of Rosebery.

**105**

**106**

**105, 106.** Mugs: pheasants among ferns.

**107, 108** Wash-basin: pheasants feeding – the HP monogram may be seen in the bowl.

**107**

**108**

**109.** a. Ewer: grouse. b. Slop-pail: pheasants. c. Basin: pheasants. d. Ewer: mallard over pond. All carry the HP monogram.

## 'One swallow does not make a summer'
ARISTOTLE

Many of the birds illustrated here are also to be found decorating pre-Wemyss pots. They make attractive decoration but tend to be rarities.

**110.** Mug: swallows.

**111.** Embossed cock vase: swallows on Wych Elm.

**112.** Beaker vases.
a. Peacock
b. Bullfinch
c. Goldfinch
d. Mug: Sparrows in flight.

*'Let the long contention cease!*
*Geese are swans and swans are geese'*
MATTHEW ARNOLD

More rarities from the world of birds. The geese are described as flower-holders in the *Fife Pottery Catalogue*, but might do well as sauce boats. The flamingoes are part of one wash-set, now split up among several collectors. The swans are painted by Edwin Sandland.

**113**

**114**

**113, 114.** Geese flower-holders.

**115.** Sponge basin: flamingoes with monogram 'HP'.

**116.** Drummond flower-pot: swans swimming on reeded pond.

**115**

**116**

## BIRDS OF PREY

Rare 'birds-of-prey' plates painted by Karel Nekola.

117

121

118

119

**117.** Gordon dessert plate: black kite.

**118.** Plaque: hobby on branch with larch cones.

**119.** Gordon dessert plate: kestrel.

**120.** Base of plate showing date and Karel Nekola's 'signature'.

**121.** Gordon dessert plate: honey buzzard.

120

## 'And lovely is the rose'
WILLIAM WORDSWORTH

## ROSES

Immediately recognisable, Wemyss cabbage roses (*Rosa* × *centifolia*) are justly renowned. At least a third of the total output of Wemyss Ware was decorated with roses and virtually all shapes were used as a 'canvas'.

The quality of rose painting varies considerably – possibly because all the decorators were required to learn 'the secret of the rose' and some were more competent than others.

The clever use of white highlights on the blooms, and the technique of allowing the glazed white pot to show through the pink petals were fundametal to the painting of Wemyss roses.

The highlights help to create an illusion of fulness in the blooms which provide a pleasant reminder of the glories of summer throughout the year. Early Nekola roses are particularly full blown, generous with thorns, buds and shading on the leaves.

**122.** Comb tray: made for the Wemyss Sales Room at the Fife Pottery and for the Wemyss Room at Thomas Goode's China Shop in South Audley Street, London, and other retailers.

# '...roses, roses all the way'
ROBERT BROWNING

**123.** a. Tiles, one initialled 'KN' (from the fireplace of Karel Nekola's home in Brandon Avenue, Kirkcaldy).

      b. Beaker vase.

      c. Vase.

      d. Rosebery vase.

      e. Tall pomade.

      f. Low pomade.

      g. Vase.

      h. Egg-cup.

      i. Match striker.

**124.** A pair of large Japan vases.

**125.** a. Wash-set. This unusual set must have been specially made to a customer's order. The authors have not seen another like it. b. Ribbon box: roses with ribbons.

123

125

124

*'Like a rose embower'd in its own green leaves'*

P. B. SHELLEY

## THE SPECIALITY OF THE HOUSE

A constant source of pleasure to Wemyss
collectors are fresh discoveries of originality
and imagination in the artists' work.
Why should one rose on this umbrella-stand
turn its back on the world? Was it a special
order, or was it the painter's professional
pride showing in his workmanship?

**126.** Gordon dessert plate.

**127.** Heart tray.

**128.** a. Tea kettle. Oval shape with
      simulated bamboo handle and
      flower knop.
     b. Cup and saucer.

**129.** Umbrella stand: note the unusual
Greek key border.

**130.** A tea-set of four cups and saucers with
squat teapot, sugar and cream.

**126**

**127**

**128**

**129**

**130**

# 'A frog he would a-wooing go'
ANON

**131.** Frog mug: this is a rare piece and as with all frog mugs would certainly startle the unwary drinker

**132.** a. Single square inkstand.
  b. Plate: inscribed 'Gollywog'.
  c. Pitcher with cane handle.
  d. Two-handled vase.

**133.** a. Ring stand.
  b. Hair tidy.
  c. Matchbox case.

**131**

**133**

**132**

# 'Go, lovely rose...'
### EDMUND WALLER

**134.** a. Egg-cup on stand.
 b. Miniature chamber-pot, a traveller's sample.

**135.** a. Bute vase.
 b. Comb tray.
 c. Dundee bowl.

**136.** a. Oblong dish.
 b. Small pig.

**137.** a. Match striker.
 b. Plate.
 c. Bowl on stem.
 d. Low pomade.
 e. Tall pomade.
 f. Stuart flower-pot.
 g. Cigarette box.
 h. Mug.

**138.** Footbath.

**135**

**136**

**134**

**137**

**138**

## 'Where roses and white lilies grow . . .'

THOMAS CAMPION

Appearing less frequently than the pink
'cabbage' rose, yellow roses were painted by
most of the leading decorators.
James Sharp obviously paid considerable
attention to the detail on the unusual pair of
Elgin vases (Plate **142**). He may have been
striving to achieve a new effect.

**139**

**140**

**139.** Footbath: yellow roses.

**140.** Combe flower-pot: yellow roses.

**141.** a. Vase.
b. Lincoln flower-pot: roses with Arum
lilies on a black background.
c. Pair of vases: yellow roses on dark
background.

**142.** Pair of Elgin vases: pink and yellow roses,
reddish bell-like flowers with visiting bees and
grasses. Delicately painted, these are almost
certainly the work of Sharp.

**143.** Basket: yellow roses.

**141**

**142**

**143**

*'A Rose-bud by my early walk,*
*In a' its crimson glory spread,*
*And drooping rich the dewy head,*
*It scents the early morning'*

ROBERT BURNS

## DOG ROSES

The most common wild rose (*Rosa canina*) in
Britain is the dog rose: not such a common
Wemyss decoration as the cabbage rose, the dog
rose is keenly sought by collectors.

**144.** Comb tray: a display plate for a
showroom, with decoration of dog roses.

**145.** Dolphin inkstand: a heart-shaped
inkstand with moulded dolphins and a shell.
Decorated with dog roses.

**146.** a. Mug.
  b. Matchbox case.
  c. Loving cup.
  d. Stationery rack.
  e. A pair of Grosvenor vases.
  All decorated with dog roses.

144

145

146

## 'The summer's flower is to the summer sweet'
SHAKESPEARE SONNET 94

In 1913, Queen Alexandra, widow of King Edward VII, was urged to mark the fiftieth anniversary of her arrival in Britain. She did this in her own inimitable and stylish way, driving through the streets of London on a day she had set aside for charity. The *London News* said: 'Alexandra rose day has come and all male London is captive at the feet of ten or eleven thousand pretty women in white, who are selling millions of roses for sweet charity's sake'.

**147.** Comb tray: dog roses, thistles and shamrock with pink ribbon.

**148.** a. Powder box.
    b. Two buttons.
    c. Hatpin holder with hatpins: cabbage roses.
    d. Perth vase.
    e. Round butter dish.
    f. Pin tray: cabbage roses.
    g. Bedford vase.
    h. Table napkin-ring.
    Decorated with dog roses, except c. and f.

**149.** Tea-set in bone china bought in biscuit form by the Fife Pottery and decorated by Sandland: dog roses.

**150.** a. Lady Eva vase: pink dog roses with white dog roses on a black central band.
    b. Combe flower-pot.
    c. Round bulb bowl: dog roses on multicoloured background.

**147**

**148**

**149**

**150**

# Thistles

The Wemyss thistle is the spear thistle (*Cirsium vulgare*) accepted as the Scottish Thistle by the Court of the Lord Lyon.

Scotland's national emblem makes a striking decoration. Notable in this group are the Thistle Vases, shaped and painted to resemble giant thistle heads.

## A Selection of Thistles

**151.** a. A pair of thistle vases painted as thistles.
    b. Low quaich dessert dish.
    c. Match striker.
    d. Matchbox case.
    e. Pen tray.
    f. Plate.
    g. Mug.

**152.** Lady Eva vase: thistles.

## More Thistles

**153.** a. Coffee cup and saucer.
    b. Covered jug.
    c. Preserve jar.
    d. Pair of 7″ square-base candlesticks.
    e. Small pig.
    f. Mouth ewer and basin.
    g. Plaque.
    h. Teapot.
    i. Tea cup and saucer.
    j. Plate.
    k. Sugar and cream.

**151**

**152**

**153**

## 'The fairest flowers o' the season'
WILLIAM SHAKESPEARE

### FLOWERS

The sheer variety of different flowers, particularly from the early period of Wemyss Ware, is breath-taking.

Most are lifelike, but a few are quite unidentifiable and may have been commissioned to match wallpaper or fabrics.

Three baskets and a Kenmore vase.

**154.** Ox-eye daisy on a yellow background.

**155.** Corn marigold with forget-me-nots.

**156.** Kenmore vase: sweet peas and pelargoniums.

**157.** Bearded iris.

**158.** a. Mug: crocus.
b. Fife flower bowl: tulips.
c. Mug: red clover.
d. Mug: violets with grasses.

**154**

**155**

**157**

**156**

**158**

*'Sweet April showers*
*Do spring May flowers'*
THOMAS TUSSER

## WEMYSS MUGS

Almost all the considerable garden of flowers painted by the Wemyss decorators may be found in these quart-sized mugs. Most have a green rim, but the earliest tend to have red rims and red decoration on the characteristic handle.

In view of the weight of two pints of ale or cider and the relatively delicate nature of the handle, one might conclude they were designed more for aesthetic enjoyment than for thirst quenching.

A selection of mugs.

**159.** a. Stylised leaves with scroll borders.
　　　b. Honeysuckle with bees.
　　　c. Yellow convolvulus (bindweed).
　　　d. Forget-me-nots.

**160.** a. Blue iris.
　　　b. Yellow iris.
　　　c. Red tulips.
　　　d. Daffodils.

**161.** a. Pelargonium.
　　　b. Lilac.
　　　c. Carnation.

**162.** Oriental poppy.

94

**159**

**160**

**162**

**161**

# 'Spring has now unwrapped the flowers'
PIAE CANTIONES

As in nature, there is little to compare with the impact of a show of Spring flowers. Many collectors choose to display a variety of Wemyss pieces decorated with the same or related flowers in order to create a vivid interior display.

**163.** a. Mug: iris.
    b. Gordon dessert plates: irises.
    c. Elgin vase: irises.
    d. Loving cup: irises.
    e. Basket: irises.

**164.** a. Japan vase: trumpet daffodils.
    b. Japan vase: yellow narcissi.
    c. Japan vase: trumpet daffodils.

**165.** Tulips
    a. Mug.
    b. Basket.
    c. Extra tall candlesticks.
    d. Loving cup.
    e. Fife flower bowl.
    f. Comb tray.
    g. Gordon dessert plate.
    h. Plate.

**166.** Fife flower bowl: crocuses.

**163**

**164**

**165**

**166**

## Sweet Peas, Iris, Lilac and Hyacinths

**167.** Sweet Peas.
    a. A pair of plates.
    b. Coffee cup and saucer.
    c. Elie flower bowl.

**168.** Drummond flower-pot: irises.

**169.** Lilac time.
    a. Hatpin holder.
    b. Slop pail.
    c. Loving cup.
    d. Sugar.

**170.** Fife flower bowl: hyacinths.

**171.** Oblong bulb bowl: hyacinths.

**167**

**168**

**169**

**170**

**171**

# '...these are the flowers of the middle summer...'

WILLIAM SHAKESPEARE

**172.** Japan vase: cornflower, large birdsfoot trefoil with oat grass.

**173.** Elgin vase: irises on a coloured background.

**174.** a. Stanley flower-pot: crimson peonies.
b. Rosebery vase: lilac.
c. Rothes flower-pot: wisteria.
d. Jug: yellow nasturtiums.

**175.** Mug with two handles: sunflower.

**172**

**173**

**174**

**175**

## 'The Holly and the Ivy, when they are both full grown ...'
TRADITIONAL

**176.** Mug with three handles: holly.

**177.** Double Victoria inkstand: holly.

**178.** Wash set with a pair of 7″ square-base candlesticks: ivy.

**179.** Ivy.
- a. Oval pin box.
- b. Beaker vases.
- c. Duchess candlestick.
- d. Comb tray.
- e. Cup and saucer.
- f. Plate.
- g. Sugar.
- h. Pair of Japan vases.
- i. Tall Pomade.
- j. Low Pomade.

**176**

**177**

**178**

**179**

*'I'm called Little Buttercup – dear little Buttercup*
*Though I could never tell why.'*

SIR W. S. GILBERT – HMS PINAFORE

**180**

Buttercups, fuchsia, forget-me-nots and chrysanthemums.

**180.** Buttercups.
    a. Sponge dish.
    b. Mug.
    c. Gordon dessert plate.
    d. Teapot.
    e. Chesham fern pot.

**181.** Chrysanthemums.
    a. Bowl with two handles.
    b. Grosvenor vase.
    c. Biscuit box.
    d. Horn tumbler.

**182.** Buttercups.
    a. Beaker vase.
    b. 7″ square-base candlestick.
    c. Comb tray.
    d. Single Victoria inkstand.
    e. Cup and saucer.

**183.** Forget-me-nots.
    a. Waverley tray.
    b. Tall Kintore candlestick.
    c. Teapot.

**184.** Fuchsia.
    a. Ewer, basin and sponge bowl.
    b. Covered jug.

**181**

**182**

**183**

**184**

# The Gay Gordons

## GORDON DESSERT PLATES

Gordon dessert plates are vividly painted with flowers and bees.

Most Wemyss shapes were named after people or places.

Among the most popular lines were Gordon dessert plates, which were sold in sets of six, twelve or eighteen (with or without fruit comports), usually a study of different flowers or fruits on each piece.

These plates tend to be particularly well painted – possibly because they were destined to delight the dinner table.

**185.** a. Fuchsia.
      b. Dog roses.
      c. Lilac.

**186.** Lilac.

**187.** a. Marsh marigolds. (King cups?)
      b. Red clover.
      c. Yellow iris.

**188.** Dog roses.

**189.** a. Violets.
      b. Tulips.
      c. Honeysuckle with bees.
      d. Beehive in orchard with bees.

**185**

**187**

**186**

**189**

**188**

*'Drink to me only with thine eyes,*
*And I will pledge with mine;*
*Or leave a kiss but in the cup*
*And I'll not look for wine.'*

BEN JONSON

## LOVING CUPS

Loving cups were among the earliest successes in Wemyss Ware. Indeed, some highly decorative, boldly painted loving cups pre-date Wemyss and are inscribed with the name of the Pottery and either Heron's name or initials. It may be assumed that they are forerunners of Wemyss. Fife Pottery loving cups were being produced in the 1870's and possibly earlier. Traditionally, loving cups were used for communal drinking on festive occasions . . . but it is unlikely that the Fife Pottery had this purpose in mind. They were, according to the late Mr J. K. MacKenzie, intended to be used as jardinières.

**190.** Corn marigold with grasses. This is an early piece and is marked 'Fife Pottery'.

**191.** Yellow poppy and stylised Campanula.

**192.** Carnations.

**193.** Pelargoniums.

**190**

**191**

**192**

**193**

# Dora Wemyss, Lady Henry Grosvenor

Two popular Wemyss vases have particularly close associations with members of the family from Wemyss Castle.

The Lady Eva vase with its wide undulating rim was named after Lady Eva Wemyss.

The Grosvenor vase, which has a characteristic piecrust rim was named after Lady Henry Grosvenor, who was Miss Wemyss before marriage. Her contribution to the success of the new ware was to introduce Wemyss to her circle of influential friends, particularly in fashionable London.

**194.** Grosvenor vase: pheasants-eye narcissus. Note the green background which shows off the white flowers.

**195.** Miniature on ivory of Dora Mina Wemyss as a child. Robert Heron named the Grosvenor vase after her as a compliment.

**194**

**195**

*'Consider the lilies of the field, how they grow;
They toil not, neither do they spin'*

ST. MATTHEW 6:28

Edwin Sandland displays his brilliant
technique on the large Combe flower-pot
... and Karel Nekola's bold, positive brush-
work is almost too much for the simple tub
with its dark blue background.

**196.** Fleur-de-Lys vase: lily of the valley.
**197.** Combe flower-pot: lilies (*Lilium
auratum*) and arum lilies.
**198.** Ewer and basin: arum lilies.
**199.** Tub flower-pot: lilies (*Lilium auratum*)
with white roses and everlasting flowers
(*Helichrysum*).

**197**

**196**

**198**

**199**

# DAFFODILS, NARCISSI and TULIPS

*'. . . all at once I saw a crowd*
*A host of golden daffodils,*
*Beside the lake, beneath the trees*
*Fluttering and dancing in the breeze'*

WILLIAM WORDSWORTH

**200.** Stationery rack: Daffodils.
**201.** Wash set: Daffodils.
**202.** Kenmore vase: trumpet daffodils and yellow narcissi.
**203.** Kenmore vase: yellow narcissi with red tulips.

201

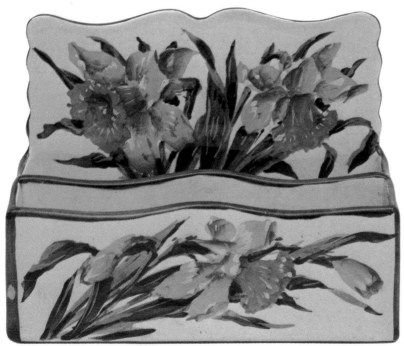

200

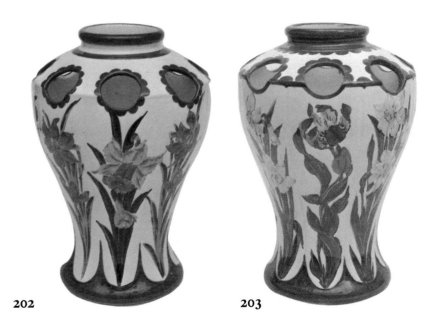

202        203

*' There has fallen a splendid tear
from the passion flower at the gate . . .'*
ALFRED, LORD TENNYSON

## PASSION FLOWERS, POPPIES and PELARGONIUM

**204.** Carafe: passion flower.
**205.** Kenmore vase: hybrid poppies.
**206.** Heart tray: Pelargonium.
**207.** Luggie: Pelargonium.

204

205

206

207

# Baluster Vase in Kirkcaldy Museum

Wemyss Ware enthusiasts and researchers are automatically drawn to Kirkcaldy. The Fife Pottery at Gallatown is no more, but many Kirkcaldy people are justly proud of its achievements. The Museum there has a fine collection of local pottery which is well worth seeing.

**208.** Baluster vase: poppy, vetch and hydrangea.

**208**

# Baluster Vase in Huntly House Museum, in Edinburgh's Canongate

This is an ideal place in which to study the range and variety of pottery produced in the East of Scotland.

**209.** Baluster vase: Exotic flowers, and insects.

**210.** Detail of painting of Baluster vase.

**211.** A display case in Huntly House Museum, showing an attractive array of Wemyss Ware.

210

211

209

107

*'Be familiar with few, Have communion with One, Deal justly to all, Speak evil of none'*

212. a. Octagonal teapot (from the general range). A Japanese shape with ribbons, roses, forget-me-nots and a verse.
    b. Comb tray: roses, forget-me-nots.
    c. Comb tray: heather posies tied with tartan bows.

213. a. Loving cup: shamrock.
    b. Plate: daffodils.
    c. Coffee cup and saucer: violets.
    d. Beaker vase: pink and blue daisies.
    e. Frilled bowl: poppies.

214. Plates.
    a. Poppy.
    b. Narcissus.
    c. Sweet Pea.
    d. Yellow iris.

212

213

214

## THE LAST OF THE PANELLED VASES

This panelled vase must be one of the last pieces to be produced in Gallatown: it is inscribed on the base with Joe Nekola's initials and the date 1930.

**215.** a. Canterbury jug (low shape): Canterbury bells.
b. Canterbury jug: Canterbury bells.
c. Mouth ewer and basin: poppies and hydrangea.
d. Keith vase: A flower resembling Fritillary.

**216.** Panelled vase: chrysanthemums, initialled 'JN' and dated 1930.

**215**

**217**

**216**

**217.** a. Sugar bowl: heather.
b. Vase: carnations.
c. Spill vase: poppy.
d. Double Victoria inkstand: lilac.
e. Oval pin-box: sweet peas.
f. Vase with three handles: dog roses.
g. Table napkin ring: daffodil.

*'I know a bank whereon the wild thyme blows,*
*where oxlips and the nodding violet grows . . .'*
SHAKESPEARE – A MIDSUMMER NIGHT'S DREAM

**218.** a. Japan vase: dandelions in flower and
seed against a brown ground.
b. Chesham fern pot: gorse.
c Horn tumbler: heather.
d. Sugar: white broom.
e. 7″ square-base candlesticks; ivy.
f. Frilled bowl: red clover.
g. Hair tidy: dog roses.

**218**

**221.** Combe flower-pot: white convolvulus
and blue morning glory.

**219.** a. Honey pot with bee knop (this is a
Bovey Tracey shape).
b. Tall Kintore candlestick: pink
ribbons and forget-me-nots.
c. Mug: Laburnum.

**220.** Matchbox case: violets.

# White Broom, Heather and Spotted Dead Nettles

The white broom wash-set, painted by James Sharp, was one of many Wemyss wash-sets bought by William Forbes J.P. for the bedrooms of Callander House, Falkirk. Forbes was the grandson on the maternal side of the Seventh Earl of Wemyss. White broom was the family's cap badge.

222. A selection of white broom
    a. Oval pin-box.
    b. Low pomade.
    c. Duchess candlesticks.
    d. Comb trays.
    e. Tea ware.
    f. Tall pomade.

223. a. Embossed cock vase: spotted dead
       nettle.
    b. Bowl: fish – probably char.

224. a. Plate: heather.
    b. Watercolour sketch of heather
       from the Fife Pottery
       decorating shop.

222

224

223

# 'The earth bringeth forth fruit of herself'

ST. MARK 4:28

## GORDON DESSERT PLATES, with fruits and nuts

A considerable range of plates, saucers, ashets and dishes was produced, but apart from a Bovey Tracey (post 1940) commission of a service for President F. D. Roosevelt, no Wemyss dinner services are known to the authors. The main contribution to the dining table were sets of Gordon dessert plates.

**225.** a. Strawberries.
      b. Gooseberries.
      c. Greengages.
**226.** Hazelnuts.
**227.** a. Green and purple grapes.
      b. Green apples.
**228.** a. Red plums.
      b. Oranges.
      c. Cherries.

225

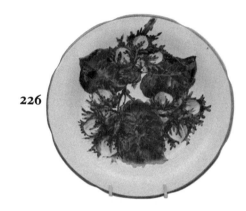

226

228
    227

**229.** a. Brambles (blackberries).
  b. Blackcurrants.
  c. Brambles.

**230.** A seven piece dessert service.
  a. Comport with mixed fruit.
  *b.–g. Gordon dessert plates.*
  b. Oranges.
  c. Raspberries.
  d. Plums.
  e. Cherries.
  f. Strawberries.
  g. Apples.

This fine set was painted by Edwin Sandland and each piece is initialled by him.

**231.** a. Raspberries.
  b. Strawberries.
  (Note the curlicues)

229

231

230

## 'Beulah, peel me a grape'
MAE WEST ('I'm No Angel')

Most Wemyss fruits look luscious and
irresistible when displayed in profusion.

**232.** a. Low quaich dessert dish: green and
purple grapes.
b. Bowl: grapes on a background of
autumnal vine leaves.

**233.** Gordon dessert plates.
a. Damsons.
b. Redcurrants.
c. Gooseberries.

**234.** a. Bread and butter plate: purple grapes.
b. Preserve jar: lemons.
c. Gordon dessert plates. – i. Pears,
ii. Apples.

**235.** a. Oblong box (for crystallised fruit): figs.
b. Lemon squeezer: lemons.

**232**

**233**

**235**

**234**

## 'Here are fruits, flowers, leaves and branches'
PAUL VERLAINE

## BRAMBLES and CURRANTS

Most bramble pieces, have particularly well painted leaves, beginning to show signs of autumn, whilst the berries can vary from unripe green, through various stages of red, to black, juicy and ready to be eaten.
A few flowers on a bramble briar are highly desirable but not easy to find.

**236.** a. Individual preserve jar: blackcurrants.
     b. Preserve jar: redcurrants.
     c. Preserve jar: blackcurrants.
     d. Embossed cock vase: brambles.
     e. Mouth ewer and basin:
       brambles. (Sandland)

**237.** Comb tray: brambles.

**238.** Heart tray: brambles with flowers.

**236**

**237**

**238**

## 'And the fruit will outdo what the flowers have promised'
FRANCOIS DE MALHERBE

## PRESERVE JARS and BISCUIT BARRELS

Preserve jars were made in seven different sizes or shapes, ranging from the tiny individual pot for the breakfast tray to the outsize one for the nursery teatable. Biscuit barrels – bearing the inscription 'BISCUITS' on the lid are normally squat but may also be of exactly the same form as the large sized preserve jar.

The problem of identification is not made any easier by the lack of a spoon slot in the lids of the large preserve jars. The 1 lb pots invariably have one; but the larger 2 lb variety frequently do not.

The authors take the view that if the piece has 'BISCUITS' inscribed on the lid, then it is a biscuit barrel; without such an inscription, it is for jam or jelly.

**240**

**239**

**241**

Preserve jars.

**239.** a. Strawberries.
b. Redcurrants.
c. Brambles.

**240.** Gooseberries.

Preserve jars with fruit knop.

**241.** a. Strawberries.  c. Cherries.
b. Plums.        d. Brambles.

**242.** Preserve jar: rhubarb.

**243.** Biscuit barrel: plums.

**243**

**242**

116

*'Cherry ripe, ripe, ripe, I cry,*
*Full and fair ones; come and buy!'*
ROBERT HERRICK

Cherries make an attractive decoration and are
the most frequently depicted Wemyss fruit.

**244.** Puss bowl: two kittens on a cherry
branch.

**245.** a. Frilled bowl: cherries.
b. Pipkin: cherries.

**246.** Covered chocolate cup and saucer:
cherries.

**247.** Cream pan: cherries, 14″ diam. The
carpet bowls in the cream pan are sponge
decorated and from the Fife pottery.

246

245

247

244

## 'A heavenly paradise is that place, Wherein all pleasant fruits do grow'

17th C. POEM

Mixed Fruit
**248.** a. Preserve jar: strawberries.
    b. Preserve jar: oranges.
    c. Oblong dish: oranges.
    d. A pair of extra-tall candlesticks: oranges.
**249.** Bowl: strawberries.
**250.** A selection of oranges.
    a., b., c. A group of plates.
    d. Bread and butter plate.
    e. Sugar bowl, with an unusual brown rim.
    f. Large preserve jar.
    g. Individual preserve jar.
**251.** a. Ewer and basin: apples.
    b. Mug with two handles: apples.
    c. A pair of extra-tall candlesticks: apples.
    d. Plate: apples.
    e. Basket: apples.
    f. Loving cup: apples.

**249**

**248**

**250**

**251**

# TUTTI-FRUTTI

252. a., b., c. A group of three plates:
     greengages.
     d. Preserve jar: greengages.

253. Bough pot: apples

254. a. Individual preserve jar with stand:
     plums.
     b. Low (small) quaich dessert dish:
     brambles.
     c. Low quaich dessert dish: greengages.
     d. Coffee cup and saucer: apples.

255. A group of seven plates.
     a. Cherries.
     b. Strawberries.
     c. Apple.
     d. Orange.
     e. Plums.
     f. Strawberries.
     g. Brambles.

**252**

**253**

**254**

**255**

## FRUIT and VEGETABLES

The garden-pea mug is an early piece bursting with vitality – not that there was ever much of a market for Wemyss vegetables.

On the other hand, the trial plate is forty years younger, painted by Joe Nekola to show the management of the Bovey Pottery Company what he could do. As with many a new venture, early inventiveness and vitality typified by the garden-pea mug, had given way to a standardised product aimed at the greatest number of potential buyers.

Perhaps this was the real reason why Wemyss Ware gradually lost its market. It ceased to amaze and delight discerning people in its effort to please a wider buying public.

**256.** Mug: garden peas.

**257.** 'Trial' plate: apples, cherries and plums. Painted by Joe Nekola *c.* 1930.

**258.** Plates: raspberries.

257

256

258

# SPECIAL COMMISSIONS

Visitors to the Pottery, and the landed gentry living nearby, placed orders for special pieces to give as presents to friends and relatives. This patronage was a vital element in the fortunes of Wemyss Ware.

**259.** Loving cup: Highland cow with a dog and a horse on the other panels. Inscribed 'Dorothy Alice Margaret Augusta Grosvenor' (who married Lord Dalmeny, later Fifth Earl of Rosebery).

**260.** Loving cup: roses with monogram 'VM' for Lady Victoria and the Hon. Michael Wemyss. This was painted for their marriage and given to them as a gift by their chauffeur. It is now in the Kirkcaldy Museum.

**261.** A group with thistle decoration and the Boar's Head of a Campbell family crest
    a. Comb tray.
    b. Low pomade.
    c. 7″ square-base candlestick.

**262.** Comb tray: wreath of violets with crown and inscription. Made for Violet, Countess of Rosslyn.

**259**

**260**

**261**

**262**

*'Lucy Locket lost her pocket,*
*Kitty Fisher found it;*
*There was not a penny in it,*
*But a ribbon round it.'*

NURSERY RHYME

Molly and Blanche
Most Wemyss ribbons occur on late
nineteenth-century pieces. They seem to have
enjoyed a high point around 1897, the year of
Queen Victoria's Diamond Jubilee.
Molly Wemyss was a lucky child to have her
very own and strikingly decorated wash-set.
Blanche Airlie, whose daughter Clementine
married Winston Churchill, had a magnificent
mug complete with ribbons, initials and
coronet. As it is unmarked, and as Lady
Blanche married in 1878, it pre-dates Wemyss
ware.

**263.** Mouth ewer and basin: pink ribbons and
inscription 'Molly'.
**264.** and **265.**
Mug: pink ribbons, laurel wreath, coronet and
monogram 'BA'.

263

264

265

'*I sometimes think that never blows so red,*
*The rose as where some buried Caesar bled . . .'*
OMAR KHAYYAM

Plaques were not made for general sale.
Those that the authors have seen have been
painted specially for friends or relations of
the owners of the Pottery, or as presents for
the family and friends of the artist.
Plate **266** illustrates a splendid plaque
showing a peacock with tail in full display.
This piece was given to Miss Williamson,
whose father owned the pottery from the
time of Robert Heron's death in 1906. It was
painted by Karel Nekola and given by him
to the young lady as a birthday present.
Plate **267** is one of a pair. The one shown is
decorated with purple grapes on a vine with
roses and hyacinth, and carries a verse from
Omar Khayyam.
These plaques, together with the two shown
on plates **269** and **270**, are all by Karel
Nekola. They illustrate well his tendency to
cover every inch of the surface with paint
when allowed free rein.

**266.** Plaque: peacock with tail in display.

**267.** Plaque: vine with purple grapes with
roses, and verse from Omar Khayyam.
Signed Karel Nekola and dated 1908.

266

267

123

*'Is this the hill? Is this the Kirk?
Is this mine own countree?'*

S. T. COLERIDGE – THE ANCIENT MARINER

**268.** Plaque: Gallatown Free Church in a circlet of roses. This plaque was painted by David Grinton for his family home where the authors first saw it *c.* 1970. The plaque has been signed D. Grinton.

**269.** Plaque: sheep and cows in woodland. Painted by Karel Nekola for his family.

**270.** A pair of plaques.
   a. Woman and girl with string of pearls, inscription *Ne nos inducas in tentatione*. (Lead us not into temptation.)

   b. Woman and boy with candle. *Quis velet apposito lumen de lumine tolli? Mille licetcapiant, deperit inde nihil.* (Who will forbid one light to be taken from another? A thousand can take fire yet nothing from frost.)

268

269

270

*'This castle hath a pleasant seat; the air nimbly and sweetly recommends itself unto our senses'* SHAKESPEARE – MACBETH

## EARLSHALL

R. W. R. Mackenzie was an enthusiastic antiquarian, a successful merchant and the man who in 1893 gave Robert Lorimer his first major commission as an Architect. This was to restore the fine sixteenth-century castle, Earlshall near Leuchars, six miles north-west of St Andrews, Fife.

Lorimer, as befitted a young man whose father had recently restored the nearby Kellie Castle as a family home, performed his task with imagination and skill. The castle, topiary and garden are of considerable interest to historian, architect and gardener alike.

Among Mackenzie's many enthusiasms may be listed his interest in breeding Shetland ponies and the faires held at regular intervals in the grounds of Earlshall in aid of local charities.

The Fife Pottery produced a range of Earlshall pieces, sometimes inscribed as such, to be sold at these faires. The designs were normally taken from features of the house and grounds and may well have been influenced by Mrs Mackenzie. Rooks feature prominently as does the date 1914, often to be found on Earlshall Faire jugs. It was in that year that a faire was held to raise funds for St Michael's Golf Club, a few miles north of Earlshall.

**272.** Photograph: Earlshall showing topiary in the gardens

**271.** Plaque: Mackenzie of Earlshall on his Shetland pony. Earlshall may be seen in the background

*'And meadow rivulets overflow,*
*And drops on gate bars hang in a row,*
*And rooks in families homeward go,*
*And so do I . . .'*                    THOMAS HARDY

## EARLSHALL ROOKS AND RABBITS

The concept of Earlshall Wemyss shows considerable originality and creative ability. One can almost hear those 'roosty craws cangle thegither'.

Possibly, the river is the Eden. Did the windmill actually exist?

Most of this highly stylised rook and rabbit pottery was sold through retailers, for the design became deservedly popular. To begin with, however, the design was made for the Earlshall bedrooms and the wash-sets were provided with matching hand-towels made by Ross of Belfast.

273. a. Rosslyn flower bowl: rookery with windmills in a sunset.
b. Tall mug: rookery with rabbits.
c. Derby milk jug: rookery with rabbits.

274. Wash set: rookery with windmills.

275. a. Milk jug: rookery with inscription 'The building rook'll call from the windy tall elm tree. Earlshall Faire, A.D. 1914'.
b. Tall mug with spout: rookery with inscription, 'Or whiles a clan o' roosty craws cangle thegither. Earlshall Faire, A.D. 1914'.
c. Basin: rookery with windmills.
d. Linen hand towel with rookery and windmills.

126

**273**

**274**

**275**

*'A little health, a little wealth,*
*A little house, with freedom,*
*And at the end, a little friend,*
*With little cause to need him.'*

The Earlshall Influence

Apart from the popular rooks from Earlshall, the castle's topiary and needlework appear to have exerted their influence on the Fife Pottery. The Little House is not aiming to be a naturalistic representation but is stylised as a sampler. The mug is covered with Earlshall motifs, as are the jugs with the topiary and gardening devices.

**276.** a. Jug: garden tools on shield, with banner and inscriptions.
   b. Canterbury jug, low shape: sundials, peacocks and topiary.

**277.** Mug: stylised design of horseman and hounds with trees and birds.

**278.** Jug: rookery with rabbits.

**279.** Mug: with stylised design, partly sponge decorated, with inscription 'Sanct Serfs anno 1907' together with verse.

**280.** Mug: stylised design of house in garden with trees.

**276**

**277**

**278**

**279**

**280**

# '...it shall be a jubilee unto you'

NUMBERS 6:24:26

## COMMEMORATIVE WARE

King George IV paid his only visit to Scotland in August 1822. The commemorative ware produced to mark this event was evidently popular and in such demand that the public continued to buy it for several years thereafter. Among the earliest known marked samples of ware from the Fife Pottery are a pair of rectangular plaques with 'Fife Pottery – 10th May 1826' incised on the back. They show a bust, in relief, of King George IV. This tradition of commemorating Royal occasions and events of national importance was carried on ...

**281.** Victoria Goblet: roses, forget-me-nots and pink ribbons. This splendid cup was probably made to honour the Diamond Jubilee of Queen Victoria in 1897, 10″ high.

128

# SIXTY YEARS A QUEEN

On 22nd June 1897 the nation celebrated with Queen Victoria the sixtieth anniversary of her accession to the Throne (the actual accession day – 20th June – being a Sunday, was marked by special services of thanksgiving in churches throughout the Empire). Flags and souvenirs were at a premium, for the demand was greater than the supply, and mills and factories were working day and night to make good the deficiency. The Fife Pottery added its contribution to the great occasion with a splendid array of special pieces – carefully painted, and no doubt expensive, cups and goblets for sale to the regular clientele. A series of rapidly painted and therefore inexpensive mugs for local children were also produced.

**282, 283.** Tall quaich (large): roses, thistles and shamrock, laurel wreath with ribbons and crown, cipher and the dates 1837–1897. Inscribed 'The sixtieth year of Queen Victoria's reign'.

**284.** a. Large Victoria goblet with decoration of roses, thistles and shamrock with crown and cipher.
b. Small Victoria goblet: with decoration as Plate 284a.

During 1980, the nation celebrated with Her Majesty Queen Elizabeth, the Queen Mother, the occasion of her eightieth Birthday. To mark the event together with the Wemyss centenary, Rógers de Rin, in collaboration with Royal Doulton, produced a limited edition of five hundred goblets, based on the design of the Victoria Goblet. Number one of the first edition was presented to Her Majesty.

**285.** 1980 Goblet: decoration of roses, thistles, shamrock, leeks, the emblems of the United Kingdom, together with the Royal Cipher. This goblet was designed by Alan Carr Linford.

**286.** Presentation label for 1980 Goblet.

282

283

285

284

286

# 'Fear God, Honour the King'
I PETER 2:17

## MORE COMMEMORATIVE WARE

During the 1897 Diamond Jubilee celebrations, and for other events, the Fife Pottery produced a series of mugs, painted in quantity and at speed, presumably for local schoolchildren or for the children of their employees. Naïve, they have an attraction in their simplicity.

**287.** Mug: laurel leaves with crown and cipher. The inscription, in letters and symbols, reads 'With heart and hand, By her we'll stand'.

**288.** Mug: Crown, cipher and dates 1837–1897 with lines and dots. The inscription, in dialect, reads 'Nae sic Queen was ever seen' (No such queen . . .).

**289, 290.** Mug: Crown and cipher 'ER' with date 1906. Decoration of roses, thistles and shamrock with linked hearts (the Scottish 'Luckenbooth' symbol). The inscription reads 'Fear God and Honour the King' (from I Peter 2:17).

See also Plates 33c, d and e.

**289**

**287**

**290**

**288**

# JUBILATION

'Festoons of evergreens, from which hung be-ribboned baskets of rare flowers . . . festooned the streets. . . . Nor were the decorations confined to the streets. Every errand boy wore his Jubilee favour days before the event. From every whip fluttered a little pennant of the national colour. Scarcely a bicycle passed that had not on its handle-bar gay streamers of red, white and blue ribbons, and even the top-hatted city man sported in his button-hole the be-ribboned colours which rule the world.' (Sir Herbert Maxwell – 'Sixty Years a Queen')

The scene was London in late June 1897, a scene repeated across Britain. It is not surprising, then, to find the symbols of celebration and joy mirrored in the contemporary pottery. Ribbons, festoons and baskets of flowers make an attractive display and were undoubtedly popular in the years which followed Queen Victoria's Diamond Jubilee.

**291.** Mugs: a pair of mugs one with royal purple ribbons, the other with pink ribbons.

**292.** Tub flower pot: inspired by the Royal Jubilee decorations? This display of ribbons, laurel leaves and baskets of flowers reflects the joy and the pride of the nation.

**293.** Ewer and basin: pink ribbons with crown and the monogram of King Edward VII and Queen Alexandra.

**294.** a. Tall Kintore candlestick: pink ribbons.
    b. Heart tray: pink ribbons with crown and mono-
        gram.
    c. Jubilee inkstand: pink ribbons with crown and
        Royal Cipher and dated 1897.

**295.** a. Part of a wash set: sponge-bowl, ewer and basin:
        green ribbons with coronet and monogram.
    b. An unusual bowl in the same style.

291    292

293

294

295

## 'Land of Hope and Glory . . .'

### ROYAL WEMYSS

The Fife Pottery produced commemorative ware to celebrate most of the very special and joyful Royal occasions which happened between 1880 and 1911. The splendid Victoria Goblet was produced in two sizes and possibly dates from Queen Victoria's Jubilee of 1887. A two-handled cup was also produced to mark national events. It may be found decorated with tiny flowers representing the national emblems of the United Kingdom. This cup, with its cover, usually carries an inscription recording both the date and the event.

The brush-work is usually of a high standard with, sometimes, an endearing lapse as the artist, realising that the internal inscription was not going to fit the rim, squeezed the letters of the last few words.

The coronation of King Edward VII and Queen Alexandra, planned to take place in Westminster Abbey on 26th June 1902, had to be postponed. The King, ill with appendicitis, was operated on just two days before the great day, to the dismay and disappointment of the nation. A great deal of money was lost as banquets and celebrations were cancelled and many dated coronation souvenirs were rendered unsaleable. Despite the fact that he was convalescent, King Edward was crowned on 9th August 1902, thus making it possible for collectors to find commemorative ware for this Sovereign's coronation bearing different dates.

296

297

298

299

300

301

**296, 297.** Coronation cups with covers: Coronation of King Edward VII and Queen Alexandra, one dated 9th August 1902, the other dated 26th June 1902. Decorated with roses, thistles, shamrock and wreaths together with a crown above a cipher. The knop is in the shape of a thistle.

**298, 299.** These Plates show the coronation cup with cover removed to show the internal inscription.

**300, 301.** Coronation cup and cover: Coronation of George V and Queen Mary dated 22nd June 1911. Decorated with roses, thistles and shamrock with laurel leaves, with a crown above the cipher.

# 'Your Country needs you . . .'

The Wemyss period in history was interrupted by two wars: the Boer War of 1899–1900 and the Great War of 1914–1918.

'Your King and Country needs you' was Lord Kitchener's slogan which called hundreds of thousands of eager recruits to the colours in 1914. The Great War began on 5th August 1914 and ended with the armistice on 11th November 1918. Fireworks known as 'Maroons' signalled the signing of the treaty and Great Britain, from the capital to the remotest hamlet, went wild with enthusiasm. Lumber rooms were ransacked for flags and bunting and people flocked to town halls, public parks and other public places to give vent to their feelings.

**302, 303.** Two-handled cup: Boer War. Inscribed 'British Arms to South Africa 1899–1900', the decoration includes Union Jacks, laurel wreaths, thistles, shamrock, oak leaves and roses. The reverse side carries the inscription 'God Save the Queen' in a laurel wreath and displays the Royal Monogram 'VRI'.

**304, 305.** Two-handled mug: thistle with motto *Nemo me impune lacessit* which, translated, reads 'No-one provokes me with impunity'. Scots consider their version more to the point 'Wha daur meddle wi' me?'. On the reverse side a wreath of forget-me-nots with the inscription 'Dinna Forget'.

302

303

304

305

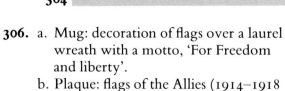

**306.** a. Mug: decoration of flags over a laurel wreath with a motto, 'For Freedom and liberty'.
b. Plaque: flags of the Allies (1914–1918 War) with motto 'These colours won't run'.

306

## 'Wee, modest crimson-tipped flow'r . . .'
ROBERT BURNS

**307, 308.** Mug: decoration of daisies in grass with a quotation from Robert Burns' poem 'To a mountain Daisy'.

**309, 310.** Mug: one mug, painted quickly to raise funds for a local need.

The village of West Wemyss lies on the coast just three miles east of Kirkcaldy. In March 1901, after much fund-raising, a new town clock was bought for the Tolbooth Steeple. The Wemyss mugs were painted for sale at a grand two-day bazaar organised to raise funds for this purpose on 30th November and 1st December 1900. The Fife Free Press report of the inauguration ceremony evokes the period for us:
At 4.30 a procession, consisting of the local Lodges of Foresters, and Shepherds, the Town Council and Committee were marshalled at the Town Hall headed by Pathhead Brass Band and marched around the Village . . . they stopped in front of a platform at the Town Hall on which were assembled Miss Wemyss, Miss Paget, etc. . . . Miss Wemyss then gracefully cut the blue ribbon which released the pendulum at twenty minutes to five o'clock and the new town clock began its public function amidst loud cheers from a large crowd of the villagers . . .

**311.** a. Dog bowl: red clover, inscribed 'Drink, Puppy, Drink'.
b. Dog bowl: plums inscribed 'Every Dog Has His Day' (Charles Kingsley).
c. Dog bowl: cherries, inscribed 'Love Me, Love My Dog'.
d. Dog bowl: roses, inscribed *Plus je connais les hommes, Plus j'admire les chiens.*

**307**

**308**

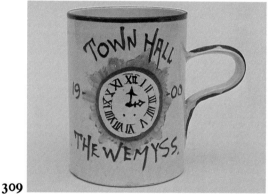

**309**

**310**

**311**

## 'Many are called but few rise early . . .'

Some inscribed pieces of Wemyss give a clue to the 'respectable' character of the East Coast Scot. Snippets of French to impress the bourgeoisie and pawky Scottish sayings in the native dialect to help establish the essential difference between himself and those born on the other side of the Tweed.

**312.** a. Cigar ash-tray: cigar stub, inscribed 'Life is but a short smoke'.
   b. Tea-pot: black cockerel in a sunrise. Inscribed 'Many are called but few rise early'.
   c. Plate: black cockerel inscribed 'Good Morning'.
   d. Plate: black cockerel inscribed 'Maisie' and dated '3rd September 1907'.

A birthday gift for Maisie Greenaway, daughter of the Fife Pottery accountant.

   e. Ash-tray: inscribed 'Who burnt the tablecloth?'.

**313.** a. Tray: inscribed 'Un regard est plus eloquent que discret'.
   b. Heart tray; palm leaf with inscription.
   c. Cup and saucer: thistles. Inscribed in dialect 'Help yersel and dinna be blate' (Help yourself and don't be shy).

**314.** Cigar ash-tray: skull and forget-me-nots. No inscription needed here. This macabre ash-tray conveys its terrible message about pushing up the daisies in entirely graphic terms.

**315.** a. Loving cup: rose-buds with inscription 'Agnes Maud Anderson 1913'.
   b. Comb tray: with inscription.
   c. Pin tray: buttercups. Inscribed 'Frae Lossie' (from Lossiemouth).

312

313

314

315

# Home truths and profound thoughts on small trays

**316.** Tray: with cupid in a cage. Inscribed 'Le mariage est un oiseau en cage'.

**317.** a. Tray: Pansies, inscribed 'There's pansies for thoughts' (Shakespeare: *Hamlet*).
b. Tray: seated smoker.

**318.** A group of six trays
a. Roses: 'No rose without a thorn'.
b. Thistles: 'I looked for something Scotch to send you and the thistles asked if they would do'.
c. Roses: 'Les enfants sont les roses du jardin de la vie', showing two children.
d. A Winter Sunset: 'Amitie de gendre; Soleil de Decembre'.
e. Violets: 'I looked for something sweet to send you and the violets asked if they would do'.
f. Rosebuds: 'Gather ye rosebuds while ye may' (Robert Herrick).

**316**

**318**

# 'Pray you, undo this button'

SHAKESPEARE – KING LEAR

## BUTTONS, HATPINS and a BROOCH

Buttons are rare and normally come in sets.
The dog's head may have been an exception, to
be worn as a reminder of a favourite pet.
The brooch is mounted on silver and painted
by Edwin Sandland.

**319.** Buttons
  a. Violets.
  b. Three buttons with thistles.

**320.** a. Button: dog's head.
  b. Brooch: dog-roses.

**321.** a. Six buttons: roses.
  b. Two hat-pins: bee and dog-roses.
  c. Three buttons: Roses.

**319**

**320**

**321**

# CHARACTER JUGS

These character jugs, showing the Maid and Beadle of Perth and the Jolly Tar, were locally popular and are still much sought after.
In 1906 a 'faire' was held to raise funds for the Perth City and County Conservative Association and a 'book of the faire' entitled 'Auld Perth' was published. The coloured frontispiece of this book is a painting of George Fell, the town officer (or beadle) dressed in his traditional costume. It is this painting which is reproduced on the Wemyss 'Beadle of Perth' jug which, with its companion piece 'the Fair Maid of Perth' jug, were specially produced for sale at this faire.

**322.** Jug: moulded in the shape of a female figure and painted as 'the Fair Maid of Perth'.

**323.** a. Jug: 'Fair Maid of Perth'.
b. Jug: the Beadle of Perth.

**324.** Three Toby jugs: jovial sailors with scallop shell base.
a. Polychrome. Signed 'KN 10th June 1910'.
b. White tropical kit.
c. Self-coloured blue glaze.

**322**

**323**

**324**

*'They that go down to the sea in ships,
that do business in great waters.'*

PSALM 107:23

## THE FISHING FLEET

Fifies, the small inshore fishing boats of the Firth of Forth, sailed from Dysart, Anstruther, Crail, Pittenweem and the many other harbours of the Fife Coast.

**325.** Ewer and basin: fishing boats in a sunset.

**326.** Japan vase: fishing boats.

**327.** Detail of painting of vase shown on Plate **326.**

**328.** Japan vase: fishing boats with fishermen wading.

**329.** Detail of painting on a Japan vase, Plate **328.**

**325**

**326**

**327**

**328**

**329**

*'I dream of Jeannie with the light brown hair*
*Floating, like a vapor on the soft summer air'*
STEPHEN FOSTER

## CURLING TONGS and CURLICUES

The paraphernalia for dressing a lady's hair
involved heated tongs and somewhere to rest
them without scorching the furniture. Various
combinations for this procedure are
immortalised on Wemyss trays – with and
without colourful flames and boxes of Bryant
and May's Runaway Matches.
The strange Eastern decoration, known as
Turkey Pattern, on the candlesticks and
inkwell, is not uncommon, but quite unlike
mainstream Wemyss decoration.

**330.** a. Heart tray: curling tongs 'warming
up'.
b. Heart tray: curling tong heater with
matches.

**331.** A pair of tall Kintore candlesticks:
Turkey Pattern.

**332.** Heart inkstand: Turkey Pattern.

**330**

**331**

**332**

## 'I've got those weary Twentieth-Century Blues'

CAVALCADE – NOEL COWARD

## JAZZY WEMYSS and LANGTOUN WARE

With the roaring 'twenties came a host of problems for the Fife Pottery. The old Victorian and Edwardian way of life had gone forever: cabbage roses were no longer fashionable.

Various attempts were made by the Fife Pottery to match the mood of postwar society. Edwin Sandland and Joe Nekola produced jazzy, multicoloured Wemyss with little success at the Fife Pottery and at Bovey Tracey.

The Langtoun Ware of the late 'twenties has a certain curiosity value – which is about the kindest comment one can make about it. Scottish readers will forgive the authors for pointing out that the Langtoun (pronounced 'langtoon') is Kirkcaldy – a local name given to it because it is a long and narrow town spread along the north shore of the Firth of Forth.

**333.** Langtoun Ware: a. Small Pig. b. Mug. c. Pen tray.

**334.** Jazzy Wemyss: a late excess.
    a. Tall mug: plums.
    b. Lady Eva vase: roses.
    c. Tray: pyrethrums.
    d. Low quaich dessert dish: roses.
    e. Leven vase: blue iris.
    f. Thistle vase: thistles.

**335.** May vase: Art Nouveau design.

**333**

**334**

**335**

*'Pussy cat, pussy cat, where have you been?*
*I've been to London to look at the queen.'*

ANON

When the Fife Pottery closed in 1930, the Wemyss rights and moulds were sold to the Bovey Pottery Company, Devon – a sister company of Pountney & Co., Fishponds, Bristol. Joseph Nekola was enlisted to continue the Wemyss tradition.

Enthusiasts have been known to fall out over the respective merits of the Scottish Wemyss and the Bovey Tracey product. In order to identify the latter it is worth noting:

1. Bovey Wemyss is never impressed; it invariably carries a painted Wemyss mark. Occasionally one finds 'Made in England' added to the inscription.

2. Bovey Wemyss never bears Thomas Goode's stamp or inscription.

3. The glazing, potting and general chemistry of Bovey Ware may be more efficient and practical than much of the Scottish product, but to Scottish eyes it tends to lack the subtlety of Fife Wemyss. Collectors should note, however, that Wemyss Ware was made in Kirkcaldy in the later period without an impressed mark, so that the existence of a painted mark only does not imply that the object was made in Devon. One must take into account the glaze which, on Bovey Wemyss, tends to be harder and usually has a shiny surface.

## BOVEY TRACY WEMYSS

**336.** A rare pair of cats 'facing': roses.
**337.** A tabby cat.
**338.** Joe Nekola putting the finishing touches to a group of pigs at Bovey Tracey. The photographer has cheated here for the pigs have already been fired and are ready for the market!

142

336

337

338

# JAN PLICHTA

In the late 1930's the Wemyss rights passed to Jan Plichta, a Czech who continued to give employment to Joseph Nekola at Bovey Tracey. Pieces are normally stamped 'Plichta, London, England' and occasionally 'Nekola Pinxt'.

**339.** Piggy bank: thistles.

**340.** Pig: oak leaves and acorns.

**341.** Cat roses.

**339**

**341**

**340**

# SKETCHES FOR WEMYSS WARE

Karel Nekola's talents are hard to define. He was a ceramic artist painting for a living in an adopted land. His professionalism and the sparkling originality and exuberance of much of his work are the qualities which set him apart.

These sketches serve to illustrate his concern for detail, colour and accuracy in his work.

**342.** Watercolour sketches of game birds to be painted on standard Wemyss wash-sets.
    a. Pheasant.
    b. Grouse.
    c. Partridge.

**343.** Watercolour sketch of flamingoes to be painted on a specially commissioned ewer. The alteration to the handle would be suggested by the management, for modelling was not the concern of the decorating shop.

**344.** Watercolour sketch of pyrethrums from the Fife Pottery decorating shop, artist unknown.

**343**

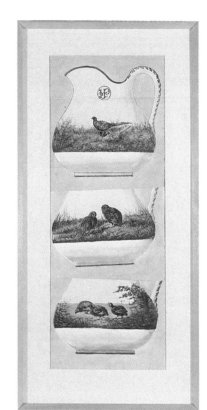

**342**

**344**

## LIVING WITH WEMYSS
## AT GLEN, INNERLEITHEN

Photographed by kind permission of
Lord and Lady Glenconner.

345. Glen House, Innerleithen.
346. A baluster vase in the hall.
347. Wemyss in a bedroom.
348. A wash set in a bathroom.

**346**

**347**

**345**

**348**

# LIVING WITH WEMYSS
# AT DUNROBIN CASTLE, GOLSPIE

**349.** Two small pigs in the library.

**350.** A selection of Wemyss Ware on view to the public.

**351.** Two cockerels from the Fife Pottery (with Thomas Goode's back stamp).

**352.**  a. Mug: pink ribbons inscribed 'Alistair'.
   b. Mug: blue ribbons inscribed 'Geordie'.
Alistair and Geordie were sons of the Duke of Sutherland.

Photographed by kind permission of Elizabeth, Countess of Sutherland.

**349**

**350**

Dunrobin Castle

**351**

**352**

*'Oh!  Yet*
*Stands the church clock at ten to three?*
*And is there honey still for tea?'*

RUPERT BROOKE

Living with Wemyss in The Master's House, at
Christ's College, Cambridge.

Living with Wemyss in the Tartan Room at
the Castle of Invercauld, Braemar.

**353.** A dresser full of Wemyss.

**354.** A selection of Wemyss Ware.

**353.** Photographed by kind permission
of Professor Sir John Plumb.

**354.** Photographed by kind permission
of Captain and Mrs Farquharson.

*'Where we love is home,*
*Home that our feet may leave,*
*but not our hearts'*

OLIVER WENDELL HOLMES

## LIVING WITH WEMYSS

**355.** Part of a lifetime's collection.

**356.** Gordon dessert plates and pigs make a fine display on a dresser.

355

356

## XV. GLOSSARY OF TERMS

| POT | DIMENSIONS | Fife Pottery Catalogue Number | Fife Pottery Early Sheets No. | PLATES | Text Page |
|---|---|---|---|---|---|
| Antique Candlestick | H. 11″ | 62 | | | 29; 48 |
| Ash Tray – oval see also Cigar-holder | L. 5″ | 58 | | 312(e) | 30 |
| *Baluster Vase | H. 20½″ | | 26 | 13(c); 15; 208; 209; 210; 346 | 28 |
| Basin – see: | | | | | |
| Mouth | | | | | |
| Sponge | | | | | |
| Sugar | | | | | |
| Wash | | | | | |
| Basket – Large | L. 15½″ | 42 | | 143; 154; 155; 157; 163(e); 165(b); 251(e) | 21; 28; 30 |
| Basket – Medium | L. 12″ | 42 | | | |
| Basket – Small | L. 8″ | 42 | | | |
| Basket – see Epsom Basket | | | | | |
| ‡Beadle of Perth Jug | H. 7¾″ | | | 4(d); 323(b) | 29; 46 |

\* denotes a pot whose Fife Pottery name is not known to us.    ‡ denotes a Fife Pottery Pot not on any list we have seen.

| POT | DIMENSIONS | Fife Pottery Catalogue Number | Fife Pottery Early Sheets No. | PLATES | Text Page |
|---|---|---|---|---|---|
| Beaker Vase – Large | H. 6″ | 89 | | 97(b); 182(a) | 44 |
| Beaker Vase – Small | H. 4½″ | 89 | | 74(f); 112(a), (b), (c); 179(b); 213(d) | |
| Beaker Vase – Extra Large | H. 11½″ | 38 | | | |
| Beaker Vase – Extra Large with Handles | H. 11½″ | 38 | | 123(b) | |
| Bedford Vase | H. 8″ | 113 | | 148(g) | |
| Bedford Vase | H. 5″ | 113 | | | |
| Biscuit Box | H. 3″   D. 4″ | 135 | | 181(c); 243 | 21; 23; 31 |
| Boxes:– | | | | | |
|   Biscuit Box | | | | | |
|   Cigarette Box | | | | | |
|   Honey Box | | | | | |
|   Pin Box | | | | | |
|   Powder Box | | | | | |
|   Preserved Fruit Box | | | | | |
| Bowls:– | | | | | |
|   Bulb | | | | | |
|   Dog | | | | | |

| | | | | | |
|---|---|---|---|---|---|
| Dundee | | | | | |
| Elie Flower | | | | | |
| Fife Flower | | | | | |
| Frilled | | | | | |
| Porridge | | | | | |
| Puss | | | | | |
| Rosslyn | | | | | |
| Sugar | | | | | |
| Bread and Butter Plate | D. 9¾″ | 66 | | 234(a); 250(d) | |
| Breakfast Cup and Saucer – see Tea Cup and Saucer | | | | | |
| Brush Vase | H. 4½″ | 123 | | 69 | 44 |
| Bulb Bowl – Round | D. 9¾″ | 74 | | 150(c) | 31 |
| Bulb Dish – Oblong | | 71 | | 171 | |
| Bute Vase | H. 12″  D. 9½″ | 127 | | 135(a) | 30 |
| Bute Vase | H. 8″  D. 6″ | | | | |
| Bute Vase | H. 5¼″  D. 3½″ | | | | |
| Butter Dish – Round | D. 3¾″ | 119 | | 148(e) | |
| Butter Tub with Cover–2 sizes | | 22 | | 57 | |
| ‡Buttons | D. 1¼″ | | | 148(b); 319; 320; 321 | 27 |

| POT | DIMENSIONS | Fife Pottery Catalogue Number | Fife Pottery Early Sheets No. | PLATES | Text Page |
|---|---|---|---|---|---|
| Candlesticks:– | | | | | 48 |
| Antique | | | | | |
| Dalmeny | | | | | |
| Duchess | | | | | |
| Kintore | | | | | |
| Nairn | | | | | |
| Square Based | | | | | |
| Canterbury Jug | H. 8″ | 13 | | 215(b) | 20; 29 |
| Canterbury Jug – Low Shape | H. 5″ | 100 | | 215(a); 276(b) | |
| Cat | H. 12½″ | 68 | | 27; 28; 29; 30; 31(d); 32; 33(a), (b); 336; 337 | 21; 27 |
| Chamber | D. 8¾″ | 123 | | 98; 178; 274 | |
| Cheese Stand – two sizes | L. 9″   H. 5½″ | 162 | | 4(a), (b). (c) | |
| Chesham Fern Pot | H. 4¾″   D. 4½″ | 9 | | 60; 74(a); 180(e); 218(b) | 29 |
| Chesham Fern Pot | H. 3½″   D. 3½″ | | | | |
| Chesham Fern Pot | H. 3¼″   D. 3¼″ | | | | |
| *Chocolate Cup and Saucer with Cover | | | | 246 | |
| Cigar-holder and Ash Tray | L. 4″ | 31 | | 312(a); 314 | 30 |

| | | | | | |
|---|---|---|---|---|---|
| Cigarette Box | | 141 | | 137(g) | |
| Coffee Cup and Saucer | H. 2½″ | 79 | | 153(a); 167(b); 213(c); 254(d) | |
| Comb Tray – two sizes | 12″ × 10″   10″ × 8″ | 34 | | 5; 38; 61; 73(c); 76; 77; 83(c); 122; 135(b); 144; 147; 165(f); 179(d); 182(c); 212(b), (c); 222(d); 237; 261(a); 262; 315(b) | 27; 28 |
| Comport – two heights | D. 9½″ | 177 | | 230 | |
| Combe Flower Pot | H. 10″   D. 11″ | 136 | | 23(c); 140; 150(b); 197; 221 | 21; 30 |
| Combe Flower Pot | H. 8″   D. 9″ | | | | |
| Combe Flower Pot | H. 7″   D. 7″ | | | | |
| *‡Coronation Cup and Cover | H. 9″   D. 6″ | | | 296; 297; 298; 299; 300; 301; 302; 303 | 28 |
| Covered Jug – four sizes | | 19 | | 73(d); 153(b); 184(b) | |
| Cream Jug | H. 2¾″ | 86 | | 92(c); 130; 153(k) | |
| ‡*Cream Pan | D. 14½″   H. 5½″ | | | 247 | |
| Cup:– | | | | | 38 |
|     Bone China | | | | | |
|     Breakfast | | | | | |
|     Chocolate | | | | | |
|     Coffee | | | | | |
|     Coronation | | | | | |
|     Egg | | | | | |

| POT | DIMENSIONS | Fife Pottery Catalogue Number | Fife Pottery Early Sheets No. | PLATES | Text Page |
|---|---|---|---|---|---|
| Invalid | | | | | |
| Loving | | | | | |
| Tea | | | | | |
| | | | | | |
| Dalmeny Candlestick | D. 4″ | 55 | | | 48 |
| Derby Milk Jug – two sizes | H. 6″ | 107 | | 273(c) | |
| Derby Milk Jug | H. 5″ | 107 | | | |
| ‡Dog | | | | 63 | |
| Dog Bowl – three sizes | H. 3½″ D. 8½″ | 12 | | 63(b); 311 | 43; 44 |
| Dog Bowl | H. 2¾″ D. 6½″ | 12 | | | |
| Dog Bowl | H. 2¼″ D. 4½″ | 12 | | | |
| Dolphin Inkstand | L. 7″ | 96 | | 145 | |
| Drummond Flower Pot | H. 9″ | 88 | | 116; 168 | |
| Duchess Candlestick with extinguisher | D. 6½″ | 44 | | 69; 179(c); 222(c) | 48 |
| | | 155 | | | |

| | | | | | |
|---|---|---|---|---|---|
| Dundee Bowl | H. 6″<br>D. 9″ | 112 | | 135(c) | |
| | | | | | |
| Egg Cup | H. 2¼″ | 12 | | 87(b); 123(h) | 43 |
| Egg Cup on Stand | | 115 | | 134(a) | |
| Elgin Vase | H. 17½″ | 39 | 22 | 83(b); 142; 163(c); 173 | 27; 29 |
| Elie Flower Bowl | | 2 | | 167(c) | |
| Embossed Cock Vase | H. 15″ | 111 | 24 | 58; 86; 111; 223(a); 236(d) | |
| Ewer | | 123 | 60 | 69; 72; 101; 178; 198; 201; 274; 293; 295; 325 | 21; 28;<br>29; 31 |
| Ewer – mouth | H. 5½″ | 124 | | 153(f); 178; 184(a); 215(c); 236(e); 251(a); 263 | |
| ‡Ewer – Tall | | | | 109(a); 109(d) | |
| Fern Pot — see Chesham | | | | | |
| Fife Flower Bowl | H. 3½″   D. 8½″ | 12 | | 158(b); 165(e); 166; 170 | 45 |
| Fife Flower Bowl | H. 2¾″   D. 6½″ | | | | |
| Fife Flower Bowl | H. 2¼″   D. 4½″ | | | | |
| Fish | L. 19″ | 154 | | 17 | 6; 27 |
| Flower Bowls:– | | | | | |
| Elie | | | | | |
| Fife | | | | | |

| POT | DIMENSIONS | Fife Pottery Catalogue Number | Fife Pottery Early Sheets No. | PLATES | Text Page |
|---|---|---|---|---|---|
| Rosslyn | | | | | |
| Flower Pots:– | | | | | |
| Coombe | | | | | |
| Drummond | | | | | |
| Lincoln | | | | | |
| Rothes | | | | | |
| Stanley | | | | | |
| Stuart | | | | | |
| Tub | | | | | |
| Fleur-de-Lys Vase | | I | | 196 | |
| ‡Footbath | L. 17″   H. 8″ | | | 138; 139 | |
| Frilled Bowl – three sizes | H. 3½″   D. 6½″ | 21 | 30/38 | 213(e); 218(f); 245(a) | 44 |
| | H. 3″   D. 5″ | | | | |
| | H. 2¾″   D. 4½″ | | | | |
| ‡Frog Mug | | | | 131 | |
| | | | | | |
| Garden Seat | H. 18½″   D. 14″ | | 49 | 18; 19; 20 | 27 |

| | | | | | | |
|---|---|---|---|---|---|---|
| Geese Flower Holder | H. $8\frac{1}{4}''$ | H. $7''$ | 75 | | 113; 114 | 21; 27 |
| Gipsy Pot – four sizes | H. $9\frac{1}{2}''$ | D. $9\frac{1}{2}''$ | 70 | 57; 66; | 79(a); 87(e) | |
| | H. $8''$ | D. $8''$ | | 86; 87 | | |
| | H. $5''$ | D. $5''$ | | | | |
| | H. $4''$ | D. 4 | | | | |
| Goblet:– | | | | | | |
| Coronation Cup | | | | | | |
| Victoria | | | | | | |
| Gordon Dessert Plates | D. $8\frac{1}{4}''$ | | 24, 177 | | 117; 119; 121; 126; 163(b); 165(g); 180(c); 185; 186; 187; 188; 189; 225; 226; 227; 228; 229; 230; 231; 233; 234(c) | 27; 28; 29; 31; 44 |
| Grosvenor Vase | | | 44 | | | 20; 27 |
| Large | H. $8''$ | | | | 102(b); 181(b); 194 | |
| Small | H. $5\frac{1}{2}''$ | | | | 52; 56(d); 89; 146(e) | |
| | | | | | | |
| Hair Tidy – two sizes | H. $2\frac{1}{2}''$ | | 20 | | 133(b); 218(g) | |
| Hat Pin Holder | H. $6''$ | | 50 | | 148(c); 169(a) | 27 |
| ‡Hat Pins | D. $1\frac{3}{4}''$ | | | | 148(c) | |
| Heart Inkstand | L. $7''$ | | 92 | | 80; 206; 330; 332 | 21 |
| Heart Tray | L. $12''$ | | 36 | | 33(d); 56(c); 75; 85(a); 127; 206; 238; 294(b) 313(b); 330 | 27; 28; 30 |

| POT | DIMENSIONS | Fife Pottery Catalogue Number | Fife Pottery Early Sheets No. | PLATES | Text Page |
|---|---|---|---|---|---|
| Honey Box & Stand – with Cover | L. 7¼″   W. 7¼″ | 64 | | 56(b); 65(b); 67(c) | 23 |
| ‡Honey Jar (New) | H. 6½″ | 172 | | 65(a); 67(b); 68 | 31 |
| ‡Honey Jar with Bee Knop Note: Preserve Jars may be found decorated with Hive and Bees. | | | | 219(a) | |
| Horn Tumbler | H. 4½″ | 16 | | 34; 181(d); 218(c) | |
| | | | | | |
| Inkstands:– | | | | | 31 |
| Dolphin | | | | | |
| Heart | | | | | |
| Jubilee | | | | | |
| Princess | | | | | |
| Shell | | | | | |
| Square | | | | | |
| Victoria | | | | | |
| ‡Invalid Feeding Cup | D. 4½″   H. 2¾″ | | | 87(c) | |

| | | | | |
|---|---|---|---|---|
| Jam Pots – see Preserve Jars | | | | |
| Japan Vase – Small | H. 6″ | 82 | 95; 164(c); 179(h); 218(a) | 20; 29; 44 |
| Japan Vase – Large | H. 8¾″ | 82 | 71; 97(a); 164(b); 326; 327; 328; 329 | 31 |
| Japan Vase – Extra Large | H. 12½″ | 4 | 124; 164(a); 172 | |
| Japan Vase – Extra Large | H. 13″ | 104 | | |
| Jardinière – see Flower Pots | | | | |
| ‡Jubilee Inkstand | L. 9½″  H. 3″ | | 294c | |
| Jugs:– | | | | |
|    Beadle of Perth | | | | |
|    Canterbury | | | | |
|    Covered | | | | |
|    Derby Milk | | | | |
|    Maid of Perth | | | | |
|    Sailor | | | | |
|    Unidentified | | | 174(d); 275(a); 276(a); 278 | 29 |
| | | | | |
| Keith Vase | H. 6½″ | 106 | 31(a); 215(d) | |
| Kenmore Vase | H. 15″ | 143 | 156; 202; 203; 205 | 21 |
| ‡Kettle (Tea) | L. 6″ | | 128(a) | 46 |

| POT | DIMENSIONS | Fife Pottery Catalogue Number | Fife Pottery Early Sheets No. | PLATES | Text Page |
|---|---|---|---|---|---|
| Kintore Candlestick – Tall | H. 9½" | 37 | | 183(b); 219(b); 294(a); 331 | 28; 48 |
| Kintore Candlestick – Low | D. 6"  H. 4½" | 59 | | | 48 |
| Lady Eva Vase – three sizes | H. 11½"  D. 10" | 144 | | 150(a); 152; 334(b) | 20; 21; 31 |
| | H. 7½"  D. 7" | | | | |
| | H. 6"  D. 5½" | | | | |
| Lemon Squeezer | H. 3½"  D. 3" | 166 | | 235(b) | 31 |
| ‡Leven Vase | H. 9" | | | 334(c) | 21; 31 |
| Lincoln Pot – five sizes | H. 10"  D. 10" | 101 | | 74(b); 141(b) | |
| | H. 8"  D. 8" | | | | |
| | H. 7"  D. 7" | | | | |
| | H. 6"  D. 6" | | | | |
| | H. 5"  D. 5" | | | | |
| Loving Cup : four sizes | H. 9½"  D. 9½" | 63 | | 1; 2; 40; 84; 87(a); 88; 90; 104; 146(c); 163(d) 165(d); 169(c); 190; 191; 192; 193; 213(a); 251(f); 259; 260; 315(a) | 20; 27; 28; 29; 30 |
| | H. 7¾"  D. 8" | | | | |
| | H. 7½"  D. 5" | | | | |
| | H. 4"  D. 4" | | | | |

| Item | Dimensions | | | References | |
|---|---|---|---|---|---|
| Luggie – three sizes | H. 7″ D. 7″ | | | 207 | |
| | H. 6″ D. 6″ | | | | |
| | H. 4¾″ D. 5″ | | | | |
| | | | | | |
| ‡Maid of Perth Jug | H. 8¾″ | | | 322, 323a | 29; 46 |
| Match Box Case – two sizes | L. 3½″ | 138 | | 53; 133c; 146b; 151d; 220 | 27 |
| Match Striker | H. 3½″ | 90 | | 36; 37; 123(i); 137(a); 151(c) | |
| May Vase | H. 6½″ | 109 | | 74(e); 335 | |
| Mouth Ewer & Basin | D. 11″ | 124 | | 153(f); 178; 184(a); 215(c); 236(e); 251(a); 263 | |
| Morning Tea Set – Including Cup, Saucer, Plate, Sugar, Cream, Teapot & Tray | | | | | 29 |
| Mug with one handle | H. 5¾″ D. 4½″ | 23 | | 54; 59; 81; 82; 83(a); 85(b); 87(d); 94; 96; 99; 100; 105; 106; 110; 112(d); 146(a); 151(g); 158(a), (c), (d); 159; 160; 161; 162; 163(a); 165(a); 180(b); 219(c); 256; 264; 265; 277; 279; 280; 287; 288; 289; 290; 291; 306; 307; 308; 309; 310; 333(b); 352 | 20; 22; 28; 29; 30; 38; 44 |
| Mug with one handle, pigs & lettering | H. 5¾″ D. 4½″ | 108 | | 55; 56 | |
| Miug with two handles | H. 5¾″ D. 4½″ | 23 | | 175; 251(b); 304; 305; | 44 |
| Mug with three handles | H. 5¾″ D. 4½″ | 23 | | 176 | 31; 44 |
| Mug, Child's – Large | H. 3½″ D. 3 | 17 | | 137(h) | |
| Mug – Tall | H. 7″ | 103 | | 273(b); 334(a) | 21 |

| POT | DIMENSIONS | Fife Pottery Catalogue Number | Fife Pottery Early Sheets No. | PLATES | Text Page |
|---|---|---|---|---|---|
| Mug – Tall with lip | | 99 | | 275(b) | |
| ‡Mug – Frog | | | | 131 | |
| | | | | | |
| Nairn Candlestick | H. 5½″ | 48 | 96 | 14(b) | 26; 28; 48 |
| Napkin Ring | D. 2″ | 153 | | 148(h); 217(g) | |
| | | | | | |
| Oblong Dish | | | | 136(a); 248(c) | |
| *Octagonal Teapot | H. 8½″ | | 98 | 212(a) | |
| | | | | | |
| Pail – see Slop Pail | | | | | |
| *Palm Pot | D. 21¾″  H. 14½″ | | 90 | 13(a) | 26 |
| Panelled Vase | H. 22″ | 3 | 25 | 16; 216 | 27; 28 |
| Pen Tray | L. 9½″  W. 3½″ | | | 151(e); 333(c) | |
| *Perth Vase | | | | 148(d) | |
| Pig – Large | L. 18″ | 40 | | 42; 43; 45; 47; 49; 338 | 21 |
| Pig – Small | L. 6½″ | 41 | | 42; 44; 45; 46; 47; 48; 49; 51; 136(b); 153(e); 333(a); 339; 340 | 26 |
| ‡Pig – Sleeping | | — | | 48; 50 | |

| | | | | | |
|---|---|---|---|---|---|
| Pin Box – Oval | | 178 | | 179(a); 217(c); 222(a) | 30 |
| Pin Tray – Oval | L. 5¼″ | 58 | | 39; 315(c) | |
| Pin Tray – Oblong | | 120 | | 148(f) | |
| Pipkin | | 91 | | 245(b) | |
| *‡Pitcher | | | 91/92 | 132(c) | |
| Plates – five sizes | D. 4″ | 28 | | 10(b); 66(a); 73(a); 92(a); 132(b); 137(b); 151(f); 153(j); 165(h); 167(a); 179(f); 213(b); 214; 224(a); 250(a), (b), (c); 251(d); 252(a), (b), (c); 255; 257; 258; 312(c), (d) | 26; 30; 32 |
| | D. 5″ | | | | |
| | D. 6″ | | | | |
| | D. 7″ | | | | |
| | D. 8″ | | | | |
| Plates – see also | | | | | |
| Bread and Butter | | | | | |
| Gordon Dessert | | | | | |
| ‡Plaques | | | | 8; 9; 14(c); 35; 118; 153(g); 266; 267; 268; 269; 270; 271; 306(b); 313(a); 316; 317; 318 | 26; 28; 29 |
| Pomade – Tall | H. 3½″  D. 3¾″ | 29 | | 102(a); 123(e); 137(e); 179(i); 222(f) | |
| Pomade – Low | H. 1½″  D. 3½″ | 29 | | 74(d); 83(d); 123(f); 137(d); 179(j); 222(b); 261(b) | |
| Porridge Bowl with Cover – two sizes | H. 4″  D. 7½″ | 72 | | | |
| | H. 3¾″  D. 7½″ | | | | |

| POT | DIMENSIONS | Fife Pottery Catalogue Number | Fife Pottery Early Sheets No. | PLATES | Text Page |
|---|---|---|---|---|---|
| Porridge Saucer | D. $6\frac{1}{2}''$ | 49 | | 79(b); 83(c) | |
| Powder Box | D. $5\frac{1}{4}''$   H. $2\frac{1}{4}''$ | | | 148(a) | |
| Preserve Jar – | | | | | |
| Fruit Knob | H. $3\frac{1}{2}''$   D. $4''$ | 171 | | 241 | 21; 23; 25; 31 |
| Individual | | 175/176 | | 67(c); 153(c); 236(a); 250(g); 254(a) | |
| Large | H. $6\frac{1}{2}''$   D. $4\frac{1}{2}''$ | 26 | | 66(b); 67(d); 234(b); 236(b), (c); 239; 240; 242; 248(a), (b); 250(f); 252(d) | 21; 28; |
| Small | H. $4\frac{3}{4}''$   D. $3''$ | 26 | | | 30 |
| *‡Preserved Fruit Box | L. $8\frac{1}{2}''$   W. $6''$ | | | 235(a) | 31 |
| Princess Ink Stand – single | D. $6\frac{1}{2}''$ | 30 | | 41 | 23 |
| Puss Bowl | H. $2\frac{1}{4}''$   D. $4\frac{1}{2}''$ | 18 | | 29(b); 244 | 44 |
| | | | | | |
| Quaichs | | | | | |
| Low Quaich Dessert Dish – Large | D. $7\frac{1}{2}''$ | 57 | | 151(b); 232(a); 254(b); 334(d) | 31; 44 |
| Low Quaich Dessert Dish – Small | | 57 | | 254(c) | 44 |
| Quaichs – Large – Tall | H. $6\frac{1}{2}''$ D. $5\frac{1}{4}''$ | 10 | | 282; 283 | 44 |

| | | | | | |
|---|---|---|---|---|---|
| Quaichs – Small – Tall | H. $4\frac{3}{4}''$<br>D. $4''$ | 60 | | 33(e); 83(f) | 44 |
| | | | | | |
| ‡Rabbit | | | | 64 | |
| *‡Ribbon Box | | | | 125(b) | |
| Ring Stand | | 56 | | 133(a) | |
| Rosebery Vase | H. $16''$ | 33 | 23 | 123(d); 174(b) | |
| Rosslyn Flower Bowl | | 47 | | 273(a) | |
| Rothes Pot – five sizes | H. $10''$   D. $10''$ | 65 | | 24(b); 174(c) | 27 |
| | H. $8''$     D. $8''$ | | | | |
| | H. $7''$     D. $7''$ | | | | |
| | H. $5''$     D. $5\frac{1}{2}''$ | | | | |
| | H. $4''$     D. $4\frac{1}{2}''$ | | | | |
| ‡Rustic Teapot | D. $6''$   H. $5\frac{1}{2}''$ | | | 4(e); 4(f); 10(a); 11(d) | |
| | | | | | |
| Sailor Jug | $10\frac{3}{4}''$ | 105 | | 324 | 21; 29 |
| Salve Box | | | | | |
| Saucer:– | | | | | |
| Coffee | | | | | |
| Porridge | | | | | |
| Tea | | | | | |

| POT | DIMENSIONS | Fife Pottery Catalogue Number | Fife Pottery Early Sheets No. | PLATES | Text Page |
|---|---|---|---|---|---|
| Slop Pail with Cane Handle | H. 11½" | 125 | | 69; 70; 109(b); 169(b); 201; 274 | |
| Soap Dish | D. 6" | 123 | | 69; 178; 201; 274 | |
| Spill Vase | | 168 | | 74(g); 217(c) | 20 |
| Sponge Basin | D. 8"  H. 3¾" | 123 | | 69; 115; 178; 180(a); 184(a); 201; 274; 295 | |
| Square Base Candle Stick | H. 7" | 43 | | 153(d); 178; 182(b); 218(e); 261(c) | 21; 48 |
| Square Base Candle Stick | H. 12" | 35 | | 165(c); 248(d); 251(c) | 21; 48 |
| Square Inkstand – Single | | 25 | | 132(a) | |
| Squat Teapot | D. 6" | 76 | | 130 | 30 |
| Stanley Flower Pot | H. 10"  D. 13" | 5 | | 174(a) | 27 |
| Stationery Rack | L. 8¾"  H. 7" | 14 | | 78; 146(d); 200 | |
| Stuart Pot – two sizes | H. 7¾"  D. 9" | | | 23(a); 137(f) | |
| | H. 6½"  D. 7" | | | | |
| Sugar Basin | D. 3" | 86 | | 73(e); 92(d); 130; 153(k); 169(d); 179(g); 217(a); 218(d); 250(e) | 21 |
| Tea Cup and Saucer–three sizes | | 84 | 120 | 73(b); 128(b); 130; 153(i); 179(e); 182(e); 222(e); 313(c) | 21 |
| Tea Cup and Saucer – Bone China | | | | 149 | 30 |

| | | | | |
|---|---|---|---|---|
| Teapot – 3 sizes | | 80 | 92(b); 153(h); 180(d); 183(c); 222(e); 312(b) | 20; 29; 30 |
| Teapot – Bone China | | | 149 | |
| Teapot:– | | | | |
|   Kettle | | | | 46 |
|   Octagonal | | | | |
|   Rustic | | | | |
|   Squat | | | | |
| Thistle Shaped Vase | H. $5\frac{1}{2}''$ | 46 | 151(a); 334(f) | |
| Tiles – two sizes | $4'' \times 4''$  $6'' \times 6''$ | 140 | 23(d); 91(a), (b); 123(a) | |
| Toilet Ware:– | | 123 | | |
|   Ewer, Basin, Sponge Dish, Chamber, Brush Vase and Brush Tray, Mouth Ewer and Basin, Slop Pail and Wash-sets | | | | |
| Travellers' Samples | | | 134(b); 203 | |
| Trays:– | | | | |
|   Ash | | | | |
|   Brush | | | | |
|   Comb | | | | |
|   Heart | | | | |
|   Pen | | | | |

| POT | DIMENSIONS | Fife Pottery Catalogue Number | Fife Pottery Early Sheets No. | PLATES | Text Page |
|---|---|---|---|---|---|
| Pin | | | | | |
| Waverley | | | | | |
| Trinket Set:– | | 126 | | | |
| Trays, Pomade, Ring Stand, Pin Tray | | | | | |
| Tub – see Butter Tub | | | | | |
| Tub Flower Pot – three sizes | H. 9½″   D. 10½″ | | | 25; 26; 103; 199; 292 | 27 |
| | H. 7½″   D. 8″ | | | | |
| | H. 4½″   D. 5″ | | | | |
| Tumbler – see Horn Tumbler | | | | | |
| Tyg – see Loving Cup | | | | | |
| Umbrella Stand | H. 25″ | | | 129 | 27; 30 |
| Vases:– | | | | | |
| *Baluster | | | | | |
| Beaker | | | | | |
| Bedford | | | | | |

| | | | | | |
|---|---|---|---|---|---|
| Bute | | | | | |
| Elgin | | | | | |
| Embossed Cock | | | | | |
| Fleur-de-lys | | | | | |
| Grosvenor | | | | | |
| Japan | | | | | |
| Keith | | | | | |
| Kenmore | | | | | |
| Lady Eva | | | | | |
| Leven | | | | | |
| May | | | | | |
| Perth | | | | | |
| Panelled | | | | | |
| Rosebery | | | | | |
| Spill | | | | | |
| Thistle Shaped | | | | | |
| Warwick | | | | | |
| Victoria Goblet | H. 10″ | | 98 | | 281; 284(a) | 28 |
| Victoria Goblet – Small | H. 5¾″ | | | | 284(b) | |
| Victoria Inkstand – Double | L. 10″ | | 139 | | 177; 217(d) | 23 |
| Victoria Inkstand – Single | | | 94 | | 182(d) | |

| POT | DIMENSIONS | Fife Pottery Catalogue Number | Fife Pottery Early Sheets No. | PLATES | Text Page |
|-----|-----------|-----|-----|--------|------|
| Wash Basin | D. 15″ | | | 69; 72; 101; 107; 108; 109(c); 178; 198; 201; 274; 275(c); 293; 295; 325 | 21; 28; 29; 31 |
| Washset:— | | 123 | | | |
| Ewer and Wash Basin, Sponge Bowl, Chamber, Soap Dish, Brush Tray, Slop Pail, Mouth Ewer and Basin, Brush Vase | | | | | |
| Waverley Tray | L. 11″  W. 4″ | 27 | | 183(a) | |